Indian Politics & Policy

Vol. 1, No. 2 • Fall 2018

Also from Westphalia Press
westphaliapress.org

IPP

INDIAN POLITICS & POLICY

VOL 1, NO. 2   FALL 2018

Sumit Ganguly, editor

Westphalia Press
An imprint of Policy Studies Organization

INDIAN POLITICS & POLICY
VOL. 1, NO. 2 • FALL 2018

Westphalia Press
An imprint of Policy Studies Organization
1527 New Hampshire Ave., NW
Washington, D.C. 20036
info@ipsonet.org

ISBN-10: 1-63391-729-0
ISBN-13: 978-1-63391-729-3

Cover and interior design by Jeffrey Barnes
jbarnesbook.design

Daniel Gutierrez-Sandoval, Executive Director
PSO and Westphalia Press

Updated material and comments on this edition
can be found at the Westphalia Press website:
www.westphaliapress.org

IPP

INDIAN POLITICS & POLICY

VOL 1, NO. 2 · FALL 2018

Editor's Introduction

The second issue of *Indian Politics and Policy* has three articles on diverse subjects and a review essay focused on three books dealing with various aspects of contemporary Indian politics and political economy. The first article, by Devin T. Hagerty, explains India's lack of a robust response to Pakistan's repeated and persistent provocations. Hagerty argues that while three factors best account for Indian restraint, the mutual possession of nuclear weapons constitutes the most compelling explanation. Hagerty argues that while a number of Indian leaders of varying political persuasions have criticized the tepid responses, India's restraint has, in all likelihood, helped avoid escalation to a nuclear war.

The second article, by Eswaran Sridharan and Aashik Jain, examines India's development assistance programs in the context of the country's foreign policy. It attempts to answer a series of questions about the size, direction, goals, methods, and rationale behind India's foreign aid programs. To that end, it specifically deals with the principal recipients of India's foreign aid in South Asia and Africa.

The third article by Kelly Alley, Nutan Maurya, and Sukanya Das deals with the issue of steady decline of surface and groundwater availability in India, especially during the dry season. To address this growing dilemma, they underscore the critical necessity of developing wastewater recycling schemes. They then examine four cases of wastewater recycling schemes that are deemed to have been successful.

The final item in this issue is a review essay by Kanta Murali which deals with three new books that focus on the determinants of India's rise to global power, examining the role of the state, domestic political, and economic resources and constraints and the role of external actors in shaping this trajectory.

Sumit Ganguly, *Editor, Indiana University, Bloomington*

Surupa Gupta, *Managing Editor, University of Mary Washington*

Nicolas Blarel, *Associate Editor, University of Leiden*

Neil DeVotta, *Associate Editor, Wake Forest University*

Ronojoy Sen, *Associate Editor, National University of Singapore*

Arzan Tarapore, *Book Review Editor, National Bureau of Asian Research*

Brandon Joseph Miliate, *Assistant Editor, Indiana University, Bloomington*

India's Ways of (Non-) War: Explaining New Delhi's Forbearance in the Face of Pakistani Provocations

Devin T. Hagerty

Professor of Political Science
University of Maryland, Baltimore County
dhagerty@umbc.edu

ABSTRACT

This article examines four India–Pakistan conflict episodes during South Asia's overtly nuclear era (1998–2018), asking why New Delhi has consistently chosen temperate, measured responses to significant Pakistani and Pakistan-abetted provocations. It argues that, in combination, three of the most common explanations—nuclear deterrence, U.S. crisis management, and a lack of favorable conventional military options—best account for Indian forbearance. Of these three causes, the nuclear factor is most important, because the other two are both linked and subservient to it. The Indo-Pakistani nuclear competition generates the urgent need for crisis management and sharply diminishes New Delhi's favorable options for conventional retaliation. While successive Indian leaders from different political parties have often been criticized for their unwillingness to launch more sizable punitive responses against Pakistan, they should instead be lauded for their strategic moderation. Indian decision making is the chief firebreak against major, possibly nuclear, war in South Asia today.

Keywords: nuclear deterrence, nuclear proliferation, crisis behavior, India—nuclear weapons, Pakistan—nuclear weapons, Kashmir, terrorism

RESUMEN

Este artículo examina cuatro episodios de conflicto entre India y Pakistán durante la era abiertamente nuclear del Sur de Asia (1998-2018), preguntándose por qué Nueva Delhi ha elegido consistentemente respuestas moderadas a importantes provocaciones paquistaníes. Sostiene que una combinación de tres de las explicaciones más comunesdisuasión nuclear, manejo de crisis de EE. UU. y la falta de opciones militares convencionales favorables—son las que mejor explican la indulgencia india. De estas tres causas, el factor nuclear es el más importante, porque los otros dos están vinculados y subordinados a él. La competencia nuclear indo-paquistaní genera la necesidad urgente de una gestión de la crisis y fuertemente reduce las opciones favorables que tiene Nueva Delhi para la retaliación convencional. Mientras que sucesivos líderes de diferentes partidos políticos han sido criticados frecuentemente por su falta de voluntad para lanzar respuestas punitivas grandes contra Paquistán, deberían más bien ser alabados por su moderación estratégica. La toma de decisiones en India es el principal cortafuegos contra una guerra mayor (y posiblemente nuclear) en el sur de Asia en la actualidad.

Palabras clave: disuasión nuclear, proliferación nuclear, comportamiento de crisis, India—armas nucleares, Pakistán—armas nucleares, Cachemira, terrorismo

摘要

本文检验了1998-2018年间南亚显著核时代时期发生的四次印度-巴基斯坦冲突事件，同时提出疑问：为何新德里在面对显著的巴基斯坦挑衅或由巴基斯坦煽动的挑衅时，持续选择温和措施予以回应。本文主张：总体而言，最常见的三种解释——核威慑、美国危机管理和缺少有利的传统军事选择——最能说明印度的容忍。在这三种原因中，核威慑因素最为重要，因为其他两个因素都与前者有关且屈从于前者。印度-巴基斯坦核竞争催生了危机管理这一紧急需求，并急剧缩小了新德里在传统反击上的有利选择。尽管来自不同政党的历届印度领导者时常被批评为不愿意对巴基斯坦发动更大范围的惩罚性措施，但他们在实施温和战略一事上应该得到赞扬。印度决策是如今反对南亚发生大型战争（核战争也有可能）的主要防火线。

关键词：核威慑，核扩散，危机行为，印度--核武器，巴基斯坦--核武器，克什米尔，恐怖主义

In the two decades since New Delhi and Islamabad went overtly nuclear in May 1998, India has been the victim of repeated armed provocations by Pakistan and substate actors supported by Pakistan. Each of these attacks has sparked a crisis or serious tension in Indo-Pakistani relations, and in each case, Indian political leaders have demonstrated notable forbearance by not striking back in ways that might escalate to a major India–Pakistan war. India's restraint was evident during India–Pakistan conflict episodes[1] in 1999, 2001–2002, 2008, and 2016. The long-standing dispute over the territory of Jammu and Kashmir[2] was at the root of the spring 1999 conflict, which was sparked by Pakistan's initiation of secret subconventional military operations on the towering Himalayan mountain peaks just across the line of control (LOC) in Indian Kashmir. After initially struggling to mount an effective military response, Indian forces eventually prevailed over the intruders with ground and air attacks that were strictly limited to the *Indian* side of the LOC.[3] In December 2001, Jaish-e-Muhammad ("Muhammad's Troops"—JeM) terrorists linked to Pakistan[4] ignited another crisis with an attack on the Indian parliament in New Delhi. The crisis was prolonged when militants followed up in May 2002 with a mass-casualty attack on an Indian military installation in Kashmir. India responded with a massive mobilization of its military forces along the Pakistani border and LOC, and Pakistan reacted in kind. Although India seemed close to launching a conventional invasion of Pakistan at two distinct points in the standoff, known as Twin Peaks, the crisis was eventually resolved without the use of force in the autumn of 2002.[5] In November 2008, 10 terrorists from the Pakistan-linked Lashkar-e-Taiba ("Army of the Pure"— LeT)[6] roamed around Mumbai unleashing a 60-hour bloodbath. The terrorists came ashore on boats before rampaging through the city murdering civilians at luxury hotels, a busy rail station, and other soft targets. The death toll was 166.[7] As in 2001–02, Indian decision makers debated launching a punitive military response, but Congress party Prime Minister Manmohan Singh ultimately desisted. Since 2008, there have been no terrorist attacks of a similar magnitude, but a number of smaller attacks—such as the January 2016 siege in Pathankot—have been attributed to terrorist groups that are known to have ties with the Inter-Services Intelligence organization (ISI)—Islamabad's apex spy agency. The most recent of these took place in September 2016, when infiltrators from Pakistan crossed the Kashmir LOC and attacked an Indian military encampment at Uri, killing 19 soldiers. In response, Bharatiya Janata Party ("Indian People's Party"—BJP) Prime Minister Narendra Modi ordered what New Delhi termed "surgical strikes" against terrorist "launch pads" on Pakistan's side of the LOC.[8]

In sum, we now have a substantial historical record of Indian decision making across two decades of an overtly nuclear South Asia, involving different types of Pakistani or Pakistan-abetted attacks in both Kashmir and India proper. During this period, different Indian political parties and prime ministers have been in office. Diverse groups of Indian political leaders have repeatedly chosen circumspect responses that have clearly been intended to limit escalation to a major India–Pakistan war. Thus, the 20th anniversary of the 1998 Indian and Pakistani nuclear explosive tests is a propitious time to examine India's political–military behavior in the shadow of nuclear weapons. This paper investigates a question of great importance for the future of crisis stability in a nuclearized South Asia: Why has New Delhi consistently chosen non-escalatory responses in the face of Pakistani aggression?

There can be, of course, no mono-causal explanations for such vital and complex national security decisions. Numerous, varied pressures weigh heavily on decision makers, and different individuals and organizations prioritize these factors in different orders. In addition, each individual conflict episode has its own idiosyncratic contributing factors. Across the four episodes, though, broader patterns emerge from India's policy choices that narrow causes down to the most essential ones. Broadly speaking, the explanations most often adduced by scholars for India's cautious responses to Pakistani and Pakistan-abetted aggression identify four causes: (1) *nuclear deterrence*, or the fear that more lethal Indian military action would run the risk of Pakistani nuclear retaliation or set off an uncontrollable escalatory process that could lead to a nuclear exchange;[9] (2) timely and energetic *U.S. diplomatic intervention* to help manage conflicts

and reduce tensions before they escalate to major war;[10] (3) an Indian "doctrine" of *strategic restraint* that predisposes political leaders to prefer nonmilitary responses to security challenges emanating from Pakistan;[11] and (4) a *dearth of good conventional military options* that would induce Pakistan to cease its provocations without running the risk of conflict escalation to major war, perhaps even to a nuclear exchange.[12]

My main argument has two threads. First, three of these four causes—nuclear deterrence, U.S. crisis management, and the lack of good conventional military options—combine to best explain Indian forbearance in the face of Pakistani provocations. Second, the *primary* factor causing India to refrain from more vigorous retaliation has been nuclear deterrence. U.S. crisis management and the absence of good conventional military options were also influential across the four conflict episodes, but less so. These two causes are closely tied—and subservient—to the influence of nuclear weapons, which sparked U.S. crisis management efforts in the first place and severely limited Indian conventional military options. I argue that the least compelling explanation for Indian moderation is the ostensible doctrine of Indian strategic restraint, which stems mainly from the deterrent power of nuclear weapons themselves, not from any doctrine or abiding principle of Indian strategic culture. The remainder of this paper is organized in the following way. The next four sections, respectively, provide succinct narrative accounts of the 1999, 2001–02, 2008, and 2016 India–Pakistan conflict episodes. The fifth section is a comparative analysis of the four most prominent explanations of India's strategic temperance in a nuclearized South Asia. I assess how well each of these arguments captures the pattern of Indian caution, explain the relationship between the primary and secondary causes noted above, and elaborate at greater length on why nuclear deterrence is the most critical factor in the Indian decision-making calculus. The sixth and final section briefly examines some implications of my argument.

The Kargil Conflict

In the spring and summer of 1999, India and Pakistan fought a limited military conflict in the Himalayan mountains of the disputed territory of Kashmir. It began when Pakistani troops of the Northern Light Infantry (NLI) covertly occupied a number of ridges on the Indian side of the LOC, which had been vacated by Indian forces in the winter.[13] By May, more than a thousand troops in civilian clothes, operating in small groups,[14] had secretly dug themselves into more than 130 posts along a 75-mile stretch of Himalayan ridges, "up to five miles deep on the Indian side of the LoC" separating Indian and Pakistani Kashmir. They were armed with "machine guns, antipersonnel land mines, man-portable air defense missiles, mortars ... and light artillery pieces."[15] Some of the intruders' positions overlooked National Highway 1A, which is the best road between Srinagar and Leh—and thus a vital ground supply route to Indian military forces both on the Siachen Glacier and along the sensitive border between Ladakh and China.[16] The Indian military discovered Pakistan's intrusion on May 3. Six days later, the Pakistani soldiers destroyed an Indian ammunition dump outside the town of Kargil.[17]

New Delhi's initial response was to send in thousands of soldiers to evict the aggressors. Special forces personnel were dropped on to ridges by helicopter. Indian troops equipped with howitzers, rocket launchers, and heavy mortars launched attacks supported by helicopter gunships. "The aim was to surround the infiltrators and choke off their supplies even while building up Indian strength to launch assaults."[18] But, it soon became clear that the army would need help. As Indian forces attempted to push their way up to extremely high altitudes—18,000 feet in some cases—they were easy targets for Pakistani snipers and gunners. Not only that, but helicopter gunships were of limited effectiveness at such altitudes. After taking heavy casualties, the Indians realized that greater firepower would be necessary to dislodge the Pakistanis. The Indian Air Force (IAF) was initially skeptical about using fighter-bombers at Kargil, worrying that it might escalate the conflict. The IAF was supported in its initial caution by the Cabinet Committee on Security (CCS); however, mounting casualties and subsequent consultation between the army and air force chiefs led them to conclude that the more potent IAF assets should, in fact, be used. On May 25, the CCS ordered the Indian armed forces to "take any action necessary to evict the invaders."[19] IAF ground-attack aircraft began to pound the intruders' positions on May 26. In the ensuing few days, the Indian forces lost two aircraft and a helicopter.[20] In the longer term, IAF operations had devastating effects on the Pakistanis' morale, as fighter aircraft pummeled their vulnerable supply lines.[21] The possibility of military operations across the LOC was a constant subject of debate within the CCS, but Indian forces were ordered to restrict their operations to the Indian side of the line.[22]

Indian leaders also tasked their armed forces to prepare for war all along the Indo-Pakistani border. In late May, U.S. satellites detected these preparations. According to one account, "elements of the Indian army's main offensive 'strike force' were loading tanks, artillery, and other heavy equipment onto flatbed rail cars." In addition, U.S. officials said later, "armored units intended for offensive use were leaving their garrisons in Rajasthan ... and preparing to move."[23] As one analyst puts it: "The key offensive formations intended for the international border, the three 'strike corps,' were 'untouched' by Kargil deployments and thus available if the political decision had been made to deploy them."[24] A senior US official recounts that "we could all too easily imagine ... a deadly descent into full scale conflict all along the border with a danger of nuclear cataclysm."[25]

Nuclear-tinged statements by Pakistani leaders fed into these concerns. On May 30, four days after the IAF began attacking Pakistani positions, Foreign Secretary Shamshad Ahmad said that Pakistan would "not hesitate to use any weapon in our arsenal to defend our territorial integrity."[26] One source speculates that this signaling was intended to caution India "against any further escalation, vertical or horizontal, in its conventional military response along the international border."[27] Indeed, according to then-Indian Foreign Minister Jaswant Singh, New Delhi perceived at one point that Pakistan was "operationalizing its nuclear missiles."[28] India's army chief during the conflict, V.P. Malik, recollects that, in turn, "we considered it prudent to take some protective measures ... some of our missile assets were dispersed and relocated."[29] Although media reports suggested "both sides moved ballistic missiles and possibly initiated nuclear weapons readiness measures during the crisis," the exact nature of any such activities remains unclear to this day.[30]

As of mid-June, India's armed forces continued to have strict orders not to cross the LOC.[31] The IAF was carrying out some 40 sorties daily,[32] in an attempt to rout the Pakistani invaders—or at least to soften up their positions so that Indian ground forces could overwhelm them. In mid-June, the IAF and the Indian Navy were put on alert, with the Eastern Fleet reinforcing the Western Fleet.[33] The navy's mission in the Arabian Sea was to contain Pakistan's naval assets in the event of conflict escalation. On June 18, Malik ordered his forces to be "prepared for escalation—sudden or gradual—along the LoC or the international border and be prepared to go to (declared) war at short notice."[34] However, by the third week of June, the tide had begun to turn in India's favor. Indian soldiers managed to retake two vital posts on the Tololing Ridge in the Dras sector, which overlook National Highway 1A, the ground supply route to other posts near the LOC.[35] By late June, Indian "mechanised and artillery divisions [had] advanced to forward positions all along the border in Gujarat, Rajasthan, Punjab, and Jammu and Kashmir." All army leave had been canceled. Trains continued to transport tanks and ammunition toward the border in Rajasthan. The Pakistan Army was making similar preparations for war near its preferred point of attack along the Punjab frontier. But neither army "made any decisive movements" of its strike corps, and New Delhi remained resolute against crossing the LOC.[36]

The Kargil fighting intensified, so did the diplomatic maneuvering between New Delhi, Islamabad, Beijing, and Washington.[37] Indian Prime Minister Atal Behari Vajpayee and his Pakistani counterpart, Nawaz Sharif, spoke by phone several times in the early weeks of the crisis, with Vajpayee telling Sharif that India would do whatever was necessary to drive the intruders back across the LOC.[38] In response, Sharif refused to accept Pakistani responsibility for the invasion. Senior State Department officials also urged Pakistani leaders to withdraw their forces from India's side of the LOC.[39] During a visit to Beijing in late May, the chief of the Pakistan Army, Pervez Musharraf, was urged to pursue peace with India, an "implicit rejection of Pakistan's efforts to internationalize

the Kashmir issue through its precipitation of the conflict over Kargil."[40] When Indian foreign minister Singh met with U.S. Deputy Secretary of State Strobe Talbott in late May, Washington agreed to take a firm stand with Pakistan, in return for which India reportedly pledged not to cross the LOC or otherwise escalate the fighting.[41] On June 11, Pakistani Foreign Minister Sartaj Aziz traveled to Beijing a day before meeting with Singh in New Delhi. The Chinese urged "negotiations and dialogue" to resolve the Kargil matter; once again, "China's non-mention of the United Nations or a role for the international community in resolving the Kashmir issue constituted rejection of Pakistan's Kargil gambit and an implicit gesture toward India."[42] Aziz's talks with Singh the next day were unavailing.

As fears of escalation grew, U.S. President Bill Clinton called Vajpayee and Sharif on June 14–15, urging both sides to resist widening the conflict.[43] But, New Delhi's patience was wearing thin.[44] On June 17–18, Vajpayee aide Brajesh Mishra told U.S. national security adviser Sandy Berger that India might be compelled to escalate its operations.[45] From Washington's perspective: "by late June the situation was deteriorating fast. The two parties were engaged in an intense conflict along the Kargil front and both were mobilizing their forces for larger conflict. Casualties were mounting on both sides. Our intelligence assessments were pointing toward the danger of full-scale war becoming a real possibility. The danger was that the Indians would grow weary of attacking uphill (actually up-mountain) into well dug in Pakistani positions ... New Delhi could easily decide to open another front elsewhere along the [LOC] to ease its burden and force the Pakistanis to fight on territory favorable to India. Even if the conflict remained confined solely to Kargil, the danger of escalation was high."[46] Deeply concerned about the prospect of an escalating war between two nuclear weapons states, Clinton dispatched the commander-in-chief of the U.S. Central Command (CENTCOM), Gen. Anthony Zinni, to Islamabad from June 23 to 27. Zinni urged Pakistani leaders to call off the Kargil operation;[47] in response, he reportedly received "fairly clear" assurances from his interlocutors that the so-called insurgents would be withdrawn from the Indian side of the LOC.[48] Immediately after Zinni's mission to Pakistan, U.S. Deputy Assistant Secretary of State Gordon Lanpher briefed Indian officials on Zinni's trip and urged continued Indian restraint in the face of escalatory pressures.[49] Then, during a late-June visit to Beijing, Sharif was rebuffed in his efforts to seek Chinese support for "Islamabad's efforts to internationalize the Kashmir issue."[50]

Ultimately, New Delhi's resolve to eject Pakistani forces from its side of the LOC, Indian military successes on the Himalayan ridges, and Pakistan's diplomatic isolation convinced Islamabad to call off its misadventure. On July 2, Sharif called Clinton, pleading for American intervention to stop the fighting and mediate the Kashmir dispute; Clinton replied that he could only help if Pakistan first withdrew its forces. A similar exchange took place the next

day, with Sharif offering to meet with Clinton in Washington on July 4.[51] According to one account, just prior to the Clinton–Sharif meeting, U.S. officials received "disturbing evidence that the Pakistanis were preparing their nuclear arsenals for possible deployment."[52] However, Musharraf contradicts this version of events in his 2006 memoir: "In 1999 our nuclear capability was not yet operational. Merely exploding a bomb does not mean that you are operationally capable of deploying nuclear force in the field and delivering a bomb across the border over a selected target. Any talk of preparing for nuclear strikes is preposterous."[53]

The July 4 meeting was tense, with Clinton hammering home both the need for Pakistani withdrawal and the dark specter of nuclear war in South Asia.[54] At one point, "Clinton asked Sharif if he knew how advanced the threat of nuclear war really was? Did Sharif know his military was preparing their nuclear tipped missiles? Sharif seemed taken aback and said only that India was probably doing the same."[55] Indeed, India reportedly had been "doing the same." In an unverified account that refers to "several high-ranking [Indian] officials" but mentions no exact dates, an Indian journalist writes, "India ... activated all its three types of nuclear delivery vehicles and kept them at what is known as Readiness State 3—meaning that some nuclear bombs would be ready to be mated with the delivery vehicles at short notice."[56] Clinton "then reminded Sharif how close the U.S. and Soviet Union had come to nuclear war in 1962 over Cuba. Did Sharif realize that if even one bomb was dropped .... Sharif finished his sentence and said it would be a catastrophe."[57] With Sharif continuing to vacillate over a Pakistani withdrawal from Kargil, Clinton grew angry: "Did Sharif order the Pakistani nuclear missile force to prepare for action? Did he realize how crazy that was? You've put me in the middle today, set the U.S. up to fail and I won't let it happen. Pakistan is messing with nuclear war."[58]

Finally, Sharif agreed to withdraw Pakistani forces in exchange for U.S. diplomatic cover. In a joint statement, he and Clinton expressed their "view that the current fighting in the Kargil region of Kashmir is dangerous and contains the seeds of a wider conflict." In return for a restoration of the "sanctity of the LOC," Clinton pledged to take a "personal interest" in helping to resolve the Kashmir dispute.[59] Days later, Vajpayee announced that "the enemy's intrusion and aggression in Kargil has now been decisively turned back .... our troops are back on the LOC .... A turning point has come."[60] On July 11, the Indian and Pakistani directors-general of military operations (DGMOs) agreed to end the fighting. A pullout timetable was reached and the Pakistani withdrawal began.[61] In a televised address on July 12, Sharif told his people "the deterioration in Pakistan–India relations brought our two countries to the brink of war .... We know that in a nuclear conflict there can be no victors .... It has been my constant effort that our countries be spared the horror of a nuclear war. Only a desire for collective suicide can prompt us to take such a

step."[62] Indian Defense Minister George Fernandes announced on July 17 that "the war in Kargil has come to an end. The last of the Pakistani intruders have vacated our territory."[63]

The "Twin Peaks" Crisis

On October 1, 2001, terrorists from JeM attacked the Jammu and Kashmir legislative assembly building in Srinagar, killing 38 people.[64] On December 13, JeM attacked the Indian Parliament in New Delhi, leaving 14 dead, including all six of the terrorists. The strike at the heart of India's government profoundly shook the country's national psyche. It was described by Indian Home Minister L.K. Advani as the "most audacious and most alarming act of terrorism in the history ... of Pakistan-sponsored terrorism in India."[65] New Delhi responded by launching Operation Parakram on December 18. The Indian Army deployed to border positions as New Delhi put its combined military forces—including those in Kashmir—on high alert. India also severed road, rail, and air links with Pakistan and recalled its high commissioner from Islamabad. Both sides reportedly moved nuclear-capable ballistic missiles to positions closer to the Punjab border.[66] The Indian government served notice that unless Pakistan reined in its murderous *jihadi* groups, India would do it for them by destroying terrorist training camps, sanctuaries, and supply routes in Pakistani Kashmir.[67] Ultimately, India moved roughly half a million soldiers—including three armored strike corps—to the parts of Punjab, Rajasthan, and Gujarat bordering Pakistan.[68] One account argues that, "in the event of Pakistani noncompliance, the Indians planned to launch rapid, multiple strikes across the Line of Control into Pakistan-administered Kashmir, destroying terrorist training camps and infrastructure and seizing territory that would enable Indian forces to staunch the flow of cross-border infiltration. In case Pakistan sought to relieve pressure on Kashmir by escalating the conflict horizontally, Indian Army forces deployed along the international border would be prepared to meet and repulse any Pakistani attacks."[69] Another analyst notes that "what distinguished the mobilization of 1999 from that of 2001–2002 is that in 1999 strike corps were not moved to their launch areas. In 2001–2002, they were."[70]

Islamabad responded by mobilizing its own armor and 300,000 Pakistan Army troops to the adjacent border areas of Punjab and Sindh.[71] In addition, fearing that its nuclear forces might come under attack, Pakistan "took alert measures to disperse the nuclear weapons and missiles to new locations away from their storage sites."[72] Early in the crisis, Pakistani Gen. Khalid Kidwai, director of the Strategic Plans Division, the body responsible for the command and control of Pakistan's nuclear arsenal, publicly stated that nuclear weapons would be used against India "if the very existence of Pakistan as a state is at stake." In addition, he pointedly set out a number of red lines that would cause Pakistan to respond with nuclear weapons if deterrence failed. Foremost

among these was "India attacks Pakistan and conquers a large part of its territory."[73] Across the border, Indian defense minister George Fernandes hinted that "India had prepared its nuclear assets for retaliatory use in the event of a Pakistani first strike.[74] Fernandes added that India "could take a [nuclear] strike, survive and then hit back. Pakistan would be finished."[75] As if to underline this point, India test-fired its Agni-I intermediate-range, nuclear-capable missile in January.[76]

India's compellent strategy was partly aimed at inducing Washington to urge Islamabad to stop supporting *jihad* in Kashmir and India proper. India's arguments were bolstered by President Bush's post-9/11 doctrine of targeting terrorists *and* the states that support them. One account says that "in the days after the Parliament House strike, John McLaughlin, then the deputy C.I.A. director, reported to the Bush Cabinet that C.I.A. and other intelligence analysts believed that, because of confusion among Indian and Pakistani decision-makers about when and how a conventional war would escalate, there was a serious risk of the first hostile use of nuclear weapons since Nagasaki."[77] On December 29, Bush called Indian Prime Minister Vajpayee and Pakistani President Pervez Musharraf to urge restraint; he also implored Musharraf to "take additional strong and decisive measures to eliminate the extremists who seek to harm India, undermine Pakistan, and provoke war." In addition, U.S. and British officials devised a coordinated strategy of back-to-back visits to the region, "with an eye to defusing tensions and postponing decisions to launch hostilities."[78] On January 11, 2002, the Indian army chief, S. Padmanabhan, issued a blunt nuclear threat to the Pakistani leadership. If Pakistan were to carry out a nuclear strike against India, he said, "the perpetrator of that particular outrage shall be punished so severely that their continuation thereafter in any form of fray will be doubtful." Responding to a reporter's question, he said, "We are ready for a second strike, yes," adding that India had enough nuclear weapons for such a response.[79]

As in the Kargil conflict, Pakistan hoped that the latest crisis would cause the United States to take a more active role in resolving the Kashmir dispute. Islamabad argued that the necessity of mobilizing troops along the border with India would require Pakistan to deploy fewer soldiers in the post-9/11 hunt for al-Qaeda and Taliban forces in northwestern Pakistan. New Delhi's diplomatic strategy was more successful; while Washington urged both sides to back off, it pointedly put JeM and LeT[80] on the State Department's list of foreign terrorist organizations. Many U.S. officials' main worry was that the dueling mobilizations of Indian and Pakistani forces would "trigger unintended escalation to a general war or even nuclear use." As a State Department South Asia specialist framed this concern: "The question was would things get out of hand and prompt one side or another to slide toward [nuclear weapon] use ... Escalation could come quickly." Another State Department official recollected fearing that India and Pakistan could

misperceive or not recognize each other's "red lines." A "seasoned diplomat" in State's South Asia bureau characterized the main danger as unintended escalation.[81] In her memoirs, U.S. National Security Adviser Condoleezza Rice wrote: "one thing was clear: whatever the intentions of the two sides, they could easily stumble into war whether they intended to or not. Those nuclear-armed adversaries could, within a matter of hours, plunge the region into chaos—possibly nuclear chaos."[82] Senior British officials, too, were alarmed at the possibility of escalation to nuclear war.[83]

In response to Indian and U.S. pressure, and with U.S. input, Musharraf made an impassioned speech to the Pakistani people on January 12, 2002, in which he condemned the October and December terrorist attacks in India. "The day of reckoning has come," Musharraf said. "Do we want Pakistan to become a theocratic state? Do we believe that religious education alone is enough for governance, or do we want Pakistan to emerge as a progressive and dynamic Islamic welfare state?" Claiming that "the verdict of the masses is in favor" of the latter course, Musharraf pledged that "no organization will be allowed to indulge in terrorism in the name of Kashmir," and that "Pakistan will not allow its territory to be used for any terrorist activity anywhere in the world."[84] Alas, Musharraf proved unwilling to clamp down completely on Pakistan's *jihadi* groups. In the aftermath of his January 2002 speech, Islamabad arrested some 2,000 militants and closed more than 300 of their offices, but few militants were prosecuted. Moreover, the leaders of JeM and LeT were released in March and promptly vowed to reinvigorate the Kashmir insurgency.

On May 14, terrorists attacked the Indian military base at Kaluchak in Jammu, killing 34 people and reigniting a full-blown crisis. Indian leaders promptly resumed their consideration of military strikes against terrorist training camps in Pakistan.[85] As one reporter vividly described the situation in late May, "preparations for cataclysm advance daily along the Indo-Pakistani frontier. About 1 million soldiers have crowded to the long border, equipped with missiles, tanks, and fighter jets ... War-fevered politicians in both capitals organize appeals for national unity ... And in the secret military warehouses of both countries, engineers presumably are turning screws on doomsday's reserve force—two crude but functional nuclear arsenals." On a visit to Jammu, Vajpayee rallied Indian soldiers: "the time has come for a decisive battle, and we will have a sure victory in this battle." In turn, Musharraf strongly implied that "if India insists on launching all-out war to attack Pakistan's support for Kashmiri militants, Pakistan is prepared to go nuclear."[86] Once again, the Indian media breathlessly reported official deliberations over military options ranging from limited strikes across the LOC to full-scale war. India's plan during the summer phase of the 10-month crisis was to "concentrate its three strike corps in the Rajasthan sector, so as to draw Pakistan's two strike corps into desert terrain and inflict

heavy attrition losses on them."[87] The Indian strike corps "were concentrated in their respective assembly boxes, ready to execute deep penetrating maneuvers to engage and destroy Pakistan's two strike corps and seize the Sindh and Punjab provinces, thus threatening to effectively slice Pakistan in two."[88]

Foremost in the minds of decision makers on all sides in late May was the nuclear shadow hovering over the Subcontinent. As one Indian diplomat said, "the idea that Pakistan will cooperate in a conflict and comply with India's wishes to fight a limited war is ridiculous. It will naturally be in their interest to keep any conflagration as unlimited as possible."[89] On May 22, the Pakistani Minister for Railways—and former head of ISI—Lt. Gen. Javed Ashraf Qazi, said: "If Pakistan is being destroyed through conventional means, we will destroy them by using the nuclear option."[90] As if to underline this message, Pakistan test-fired three nuclear-capable ballistic missiles, which the Indians interpreted "as a warning ... to apply brakes on India's most ambitious plan ever."[91] Musharraf claimed that the tests "validated the reliability, accuracy, and ... deterrence value of Pakistan's premier surface-to-surface ballistic missile systems."[92] On May 29, Pakistan's ambassador to the United Nations defended his country's refusal to adopt a no-first-use nuclear posture by asking rhetorically: "How can Pakistan, a weaker power, be expected to rule out all means of deterrence?"[93] In Washington, Secretary of State Colin Powell and Deputy Secretary of State Richard Armitage "worried ... about the nuclear dimension of the crisis." One source reports that "the situation from late May onward appeared sufficiently bleak for the Pentagon to reexamine the effects of nuclear weapons' use on the Subcontinent. One official vividly remembers interagency discussions ... on evacuating the embassies and U.S. nationals in the event of a nuclear exchange. The Subcontinent's seasonal 'plumology' was studied." U.S. Embassy staff in both New Delhi and Islamabad worried about the possibility of the crisis escalating to nuclear war.[94] Asked in early June if his government had considered the possibility of war escalating to the use of nuclear weapons, Indian Defense Secretary Yogendra Narain replied, "Certainly. But we don't know [Pakistan's] nuclear threshold. We will retaliate and must be prepared for mutual destruction on both sides."[95] All in all, reports one authoritative account, "Washington's regional specialists were nearly unanimous in predicting that war was ... imminent. They saw no obvious pathway for the two governments to walk back from the brink."[96] A senior U.S. intelligence analyst with years of regional experience told the author in early June 2002 that he estimated the chances of India-Pakistan war at "100 percent."

With Pakistan sending "many signals to Delhi that any invasion of Pakistan would warrant a Pakistani nuclear response,"[97] Washington began another flurry of diplomatic activity to prevent war in South Asia. The State Department also issued a travel advisory urging U.S. citizens to leave India.[98] On June 6, Armitage went to Islamabad,

where he reportedly elicited a promise from Musharraf to "end cross-border infiltration permanently."[99] Armitage relayed this pledge to Indian officials in New Delhi the next day. Two weeks later, though, Musharraf seemed to backtrack when he told a reporter, "I'm not going to give you an assurance that for years nothing will happen."[100] That said, infiltrations across the LOC did decrease during the summer before rising again in the autumn, "but not to the level that they had been at previously, prior to the commitments made by the Pakistani government."[101] Although the immediate crisis faded in June, the Indo-Pakistani troop buildup lasted until October, when India announced that it would withdraw its forces from the border with Pakistan. The Indian decision came on the heels of state elections in Kashmir, after which "there was no reason to continue a deployment that has placed enormous strains on personnel, equipment, and morale."[102] Pakistan immediately reciprocated the troop withdrawal. All sides agree that India and Pakistan nearly fought a major war in the summer of 2002. Musharraf said war was "very close." Vajpayee called it "a touch-and-go affair." U.S. Assistant Secretary of State for South Asian affairs Christina Rocca stated that the two sides had "barely averted war."[103]

The 26/11 Mumbai Terrorist Attacks

On November 26, 2008, 10 LeT terrorists went on a killing spree in Mumbai, India's commercial capital and second-largest city.

Armed with AK-56 automatic assault rifles, pistols, hand grenades, and improvised explosive devices (IEDs), and supplied with satellite phones and GPS sets,[104] they murdered 166 people[105] and wounded more than 300 in a 60-hour rampage. They departed from Karachi by boat, hijacked an Indian vessel at sea, arrived in Mumbai under cover of darkness, split into four teams, and systematically carried out their assaults at multiple locations, including the luxury Oberoi-Trident and Taj Mahal Palace hotels; a major railroad station, the Chhatrapati Shivaji Terminus; a high-end restaurant popular with tourists, the Leopold Cafe; and a hostel run by the Jewish Chabad-Lubavich movement.[106] The terrorists were directed during the attacks in real time by LeT handlers in Pakistan, and live television coverage added to the shock value of the assaults. Similar to the way Americans remember "9/11," Indians recall the Mumbai carnage simply as "26/11." The attacks did not ignite a full-blown crisis like Twin Peaks; nor did they set off an Indo-Pakistani military conflict like Kargil. However, "there was a sense of crisis, even if less severe than in previous confrontations."[107] A subsequent U.S. Ambassador to India, Timothy Roemer, said of 26/11: "[the terrorists] almost started a war between Pakistan and India that might have resulted in some kind of a nuclear war."[108] At a minimum, the massacre generated extreme pressure on the government of Prime Minister Manmohan Singh to retaliate against Pakistan with military force, which in turn stoked escalating Indo-Pakistani tensions.[109] The U.S. ambassador to India at the time of

the attacks, David Mulford, characterized the prevailing atmosphere in New Delhi as "war fever."[110]

The aura of looming confrontation was intensified by a bizarre incident on November 28, while the attacks were ongoing. A person claiming to be Indian External Affairs Minister Pranab Mukherjee made a telephone call to Pakistan's president, Asif Ali Zardari, in which the caller threatened war.[111] Then-U.S. Secretary of State Condoleezza Rice recalls being told by a National Security Council (NSC) staffer the next day that "the Pakistanis say the Indians have warned them that they've decided to go to war." Rice was surprised to hear this, as Indian officials had been emphasizing "their desire to defuse the situation." When she finally reached Mukherjee by telephone, he was away from New Delhi campaigning in his constituency. He said to her: "Would I be outside New Delhi if we were about to launch a war?"[112] For U.S. officials, the mysterious telephone call "conjured the specter of Pakistani military action to preempt a feared Indian attack." One NSC official recollected that "the fake phone call recounted by Pak officials changed everything—risked having all spin out of control. The key was that we were confident that India did not say this [that India was preparing to attack Pakistan], but they [Pakistani officials] were all ramped up. Our job was to bring them down."[113]

Discussions between Indian leaders focused on India's "options, the likely Pakistani response, and the escalation that could occur."[114] Senior national-security officials met on November 29, the last day of the bloodshed, to discuss possible Indian responses. The gravity of the situation was reflected in the meeting's roster of attendees, which included Prime Minister Singh, the Defense Minister, the National Security Adviser, the heads of India's two intelligence agencies, and the service chiefs.[115] Although Singh made it clear at the outset that he was not in favor of another massive mobilization of forces like Operation Parakram in 2001–02, more limited military options were thoroughly discussed.[116] Air Chief Marshall Fali Major reportedly "suggested striking terrorist camps" on Pakistan's side of the LOC in Kashmir.[117] Another credible account of the meeting says that while Major did say that Indian ground-attack aircraft could hit training camps across the LOC, he added that "precise coordinates and adequate imaging weren't available."[118] Missile strikes against Pakistani targets were another option, but "no one could guarantee missile strikes wouldn't escalate into war, or even a nuclear exchange."[119] As for potential ground operations, Chief of Army Staff (COAS) Kapoor subsequently raised the possibility of a limited ground strike approximately 10–15 kilometers into Pakistani Punjab.[120] According to one account, however, both he and Major "made it clear that they lacked the wherewithal for war if Pakistan decided to escalate matters, adding that the Pakistan Army was unlikely to not retaliate."[121] Kapoor also told Singh that special forces operations might well fail.[122] In another meeting between Defense Minister A.K. Antony and the service chiefs, Antony asked Kapoor again about the prospect

of limited ground strikes. One reliable account has it that "Gen. Kapoor is said to have responded that an operation was possible but he would need a week's notice and that it would be a 'highly risky' affair .... In the Army's assessment, any strike would definitely lead to an escalated military conflict and the government ought to be prepared for it. The air force agreed that a strong Pakistani reaction was certain."[123] Covert operations were also discussed, but the Research and Analysis Wing (RAW), India's external intelligence agency "admitted that it had no assets in Pakistan to carry out such an action."[124]

In sum, secret Indian deliberations about the use of force in response to the 26/11 attacks were characterized by deep uncertainty about the likelihood and nature of Pakistani retaliation, leavened with worst-case expectations of significant escalation potential. One thorough study of the 26/11 episode argues that "Indian officials were genuinely conflicted about how to respond to Pakistan. They certainly did not want to risk a nuclear exchange. They also wanted to avoid undercutting a new and fragile civilian government .... But they did not want their country to appear weak."[125] As a consequence of this dilemma, senior Indian officials signaled mixed messages regarding their intentions, especially in the early days following the attacks. On the one hand, they periodically issued warnings that all options, including military ones, were on the table.[126] Accompanying these signals were stern pronouncements, such as Mukherjee's veiled threat that "we are determined to take the strongest possible measures to ensure that there is no repetition of such acts."[127] On the other hand, Indian officials repeatedly maintained that the political leadership had decided against military action.[128] Meanwhile, reputable media accounts in early December tended to focus on the possibility of so-called surgical strikes against "militant infrastructure" in Pakistani Kashmir, even as prominent national-security figures weighed in with warnings about the dangerous consequences of even limited attacks.[129] Across the border, Pakistani leaders, uncertain which of these messages were authentic, grew fearful that India was gearing up for a military response and braced themselves for an attack.[130] One retrospective account suggests that both the Indian and Pakistani air forces raised their alert levels "during and immediately after the attacks," and that Pakistan put its "advance ground units on alert."[131] Pakistan's concerns about Indian military action drove esteemed nuclear scientist Samar Mubarakmand to note in a television interview that Pakistan was "capable of launching a nuclear missile against India with ten minutes' notice," and that "the force that launched first had an advantage."[132]

As in 1999 and 2001–02, U.S. policymakers were quick to mobilize in an effort to prevent Indo-Pakistani tensions from spiraling into a full-blown crisis or even war. Within 24 hours of the attacks, President Bush had spoken with both the Indian and Pakistani leaders by telephone. He counseled restraint and offered investigative resources to India. The administration also began to coordinate with President-elect Barack Obama, who would inherit the aftermath of the crisis in January 2009.[133] A Federal Bureau of Investigation (FBI) team arrived in Mumbai on December 1.[134] U.S. decision makers initially feared that India might carry out air strikes on LeT camps in Pakistan. LeT's "home base" was in Muridke, Punjab, in a heavily populated area about 20 miles north of Lahore. Said one official: "It would have meant a conventional war or worse. Plus the bad guys would have been long gone."[135] Another concern was that Pakistan might try to preempt limited Indian Army thrusts across the international border, often referred to under the moniker of "Cold Start."[136] U.S. analysts tried hard to read Indian intentions as the confrontation unfolded, but their view inside the CCS was "incredibly murky."[137] As one granular narrative summarizes U.S. perceptions: "The Mumbai attacks sparked concerns about a replay of escalatory actions by India and Pakistan" during the Twin Peaks crisis. "Indian officials were ... blaming Pakistan for the attacks. Any conflict between the two nuclear-armed neighbors could get out of hand. Pakistani leaders vowed to respond to any attack by India as a threat to Pakistan's sovereignty and survival, while Indian leaders pointedly did not take off the table limited-war scenarios."[138]

Senior U.S. officials also traveled to the region to meet with their Indian and Pakistani counterparts. Secretary Rice interrupted a trip to Europe to meet with Mukherjee on December 3. She cautioned New Delhi against actions that might produce "unintended consequences." At the same time, Adm. Michael Mullen, Chairman of the Joint Chiefs of Staff (JCS), was in Islamabad meeting with President Zardari and COAS Ashfaq Parvez Kayani. Rice then traveled from India to Pakistan, where she met with Zardari, Kayani, Prime Minister Yousuf Raza Gilani, and Foreign Minister Shah Mahmood Qureshi.[139] Immediately after the Mumbai attacks, India had demanded that Pakistan apprehend 20 high-profile terrorist suspects and extradite them to India for trial.[140] Rice and Mullen complemented that message by urging their Pakistani interlocutors to aggressively investigate and bring to justice those responsible for the carnage, with Rice adding that there was "irrefutable evidence" that Pakistani nationals were involved in the massacre.[141] Days later, U.S. Sen. John McCain, visiting Islamabad after talks in New Delhi, warned Pakistani leaders that India "would be left with no choice but to carry out surgical strikes against" targets linked to the Mumbai attacks unless Pakistan cracked down on terrorist elements.[142] In sum, U.S. crisis-management priorities in early December were to convince New Delhi not to respond militarily to 26/11, and to "get the Pakistanis to cough up people and clamp down [on terrorists]." In response, Islamabad—which denied any connection to the Mumbai tragedy—went through the motions of arresting 22 LeT members, banning LeT affiliate Jamaat-ud-Dawa ("Society for Proselytization"—JuD), and putting LeT/JuD leader Hafiz Saeed under house arrest. But, there was "no systematic crackdown on LeT's infra-

structure and apparatus in Pakistan."[143]

A week after the LeT attacks, it looked as though the danger of a major crisis had been contained. An Indian diplomat emphasized to his counterparts in the U.S. embassy in Islamabad that "India has issued no war warnings to Pakistan and had not mobilized its forces."[144] Indian Foreign Secretary Shivshankar Menon subsequently told U.S. diplomats that "India, in the wake of the Mumbai attacks, had consciously not built up troops on the border, as it had following the 2001 attack on its Parliament."[145] New Delhi did, however, put on hold the "Composite Dialogue," a diplomatic process begun in 2004 that had generated some momentum in attempting to resolve a number of India–Pakistan political conflicts. As U.S. diplomats in New Delhi explained, "the Mumbai terrorist attacks deeply angered the Indian public. This time, in addition to the reactions against Pakistan, Indians directed a new level of fury at their own political establishment, which they feel failed to protect them." The "public's anger pushed" Prime Minister Singh to "shelve" the dialogue.[146] In a forceful speech in Parliament on December 11, Singh described Pakistan as the "epicenter of terrorism," warned that Indian restraint should not be "misconstrued as a sign of weakness," and demanded that the "infrastructure of terrorism" in Pakistan be "dismantled permanently." But, the bulk of the prime minister's speech focused on the necessity of domestic security reforms and improving future efforts to prevent attacks.[147] Generally speaking, New Delhi's "focus was primarily on domestic security measures, rather than on military action or on coercive threats aimed at Pakistan .... The Indians took no rhetorical or military steps to threaten to attack Pakistan as they did during the 2001–2002 crisis."[148]

Still, tension lingered into mid-December and beyond. Islamabad claimed that Indian fighter jets violated Pakistani airspace on December 13.[149] Alongside media reports that "Indian air force units were placed on alert for possible strikes on suspected terrorist camps inside Pakistan,"[150] this heightened the tension among Pakistani decision makers. The Pakistan Air Force (PAF) carried out exercises over major northern cities and Kashmir on December 22, and on December 23, the head of India's Western Air Command, Air Marshal P.K. Barbora, said that India had "earmarked" 5,000 Pakistani targets for air strikes.[151] At the same time, Pakistani COAS Kayani warned that Pakistani military forces would "retaliate within minutes" if India carried out a surgical strike within Pakistan.[152] In late December, the Indian Army extended the presence of two brigades in Rajasthan after scheduled seasonal exercises.[153] In response, Islamabad moved some 5,000–7,000 troops from the Federally Administered Tribal Areas (FATA), bordering Afghanistan, eastward to positions along the LOC and the Punjab frontier.[154] Senior Pakistani officials asked the Indian side to pull its forces back from the border area, and repeated that Pakistan would meet any Indian aggression, even surgical strikes, with quick retaliation. Still, the two sides continued to communicate direct-

ly in an effort to ease the tension. On December 26, for example, the Indian High Commissioner in Islamabad told the Pakistani foreign secretary "that India had no plans to go to war."[155] With the arrival of the new year, hostilities gradually abated. India had once again chosen not to retaliate militarily in the face of egregious provocation by Pakistan-based terrorists.

The Uri Attack and Indian "Surgical Strikes"

In the pre-dawn hours of September 18, 2016, four guerrillas from Pakistan attacked an Indian army encampment roughly 6 kilometers from the LOC. The attackers, armed with grenades and assault rifles, slaughtered 19 Indian soldiers and wounded 20, before themselves being killed in a 3-hour gun battle. The scene of the carnage, a brigade headquarters, was unusually crowded at the time with two battalions of soldiers rotating in and out. Many of the casualties had been sleeping in tents and other temporary shelters, which quickly caught fire when the attackers used incendiary ammunition. The assault at Uri was India's largest mass-casualty attack since Mumbai in 2008 and the deadliest raid on an Indian base in Kashmir since 2002. It was carried out in the context of a rapidly deteriorating security situation in Indian Kashmir since the July 8 killing of a Hizbul Mujahideen commander, Burhan Wani, in a shootout with security forces. Since Wani's death, more than 80 people had been killed and thousands more wounded in hostilities between protesters and government forces. The attack also followed on the heels of cross-border strikes on an Indian police station at Gurdaspur in July 2015 and an IAF base at Pathankot in January 2016, both in Punjab. Seven Indians were killed in each of those assaults.[156]

The Uri massacre caused an outcry in India. The number of dead and wounded, and the gruesome manner in which they were killed or injured, generated heated demands for a punitive response by the BJP government of Prime Minister Narendra Modi. Elected in 2014, Modi had offered Pakistan several olive branches in an attempt to stabilize Indo-Pakistani relations, but his efforts had come to naught. Modi had been critical of the previous government of Manmohan Singh for not retaliating more forcefully to Pakistani provocations like the Mumbai attacks of 2008. Modi's supporters strongly approved of his more muscular disposition, and the Indian media in Uri's aftermath were filled with breathless speculation about strikes against "terrorist infrastructure" on the Pakistani side of the LOC. Hours after the attack, Modi pledged that "those behind this despicable act will not go unpunished." The BJP's national general secretary, Ram Madhav, added fuel to the fire by declaring: "For one tooth, the complete jaw. [The] days of so-called strategic restraint are over." India's DGMO said that the attackers were "foreign terrorists" whose weapons had "Pakistani markings."[157] Indian home minister Rajnath Singh was more explicit, tweeting that: "Pakistan is a terrorist state."[158]

As in previous crises, India's national-security leadership gathered quickly to discuss "possible long-term options to retaliate against jihadist logistics and the Pakistani military infrastructure." In a September 19 meeting at Modi's residence, the prime minister, home minister Singh, Defense Minister Manohar Parrikar, Finance Minister Arun Jaitley, and National Security Adviser Ajit Doval were told by the senior military leadership that Pakistan had "raised its defensive posture along the LOC" by "fortifying its positions," making an Indian military response risky."[159] On September 22, the Indian DGMO, Lt. Gen. Ranbir Singh, briefed Modi and his national security team more specifically on "LOC strike options."[160] An American analyst captured the dilemma faced by New Delhi: "India still lacks military options that could satisfy its strategic objectives, the first of which is to get the Pakistani army to demobilize the most potent anti-India militant groups." Punitive retaliation "robust enough to really harm the Pakistani military could also leave that military unwilling and unable to demobilize the most potent anti-India militants in Pakistan. And even if Indian forces had the ability to move into Pakistani territory to inflict major damage on the army, Pakistan could use its nuclear weapons to stave off defeat. ... But a restrained use of force could signal lack of Indian resolve, thereby emboldening the Pakistani military."[161]

Meanwhile, Pakistan's leadership vigorously denied any involvement in the Uri attack, instead criticizing New Delhi for the ongoing violence in Kashmir. In a speech before the U.N. General Assembly (UNGA) on September 21, Prime Minister Nawaz Sharif argued that "a new generation of Kashmiris has risen spontaneously against India's illegal occupation—demanding freedom from occupation. Burhan Wani, the young leader murdered by Indian forces, has emerged as the symbol of the latest Kashmiri intifada," while New Delhi has responded with "brutal repression by India's occupation force of over half a million soldiers."[162] During the UNGA meeting in New York, U.S. Secretary of State John Kerry met with both Sharif and Indian External Affairs Minister Sushma Swaraj, urging them to avoid escalating the conflict in Kashmir.[163] At home, Pakistani leaders girded themselves for a potential Indian attack, while at the same time issuing their by-now characteristic nuclear deterrence threats. Army chief Raheel Sharif said that his forces were in their "highest state of vigilance" along the border.[164] PAF fighter aircraft practiced takeoffs and landings on a major six-lane highway connecting Islamabad and Lahore, in the process blocking traffic and closing commercial airspace. Although officials characterized this as a "routine" air defense exercise, it was anything but.[165] Meanwhile, in a September 26 television interview, Pakistan's Defense Minister, Khawaja Muhammad Asif said: "Tactical [nuclear] weapons, our programmes that we have developed, they have been developed for our protection. We haven't kept the devices that we have just as showpieces. But if our safety is threatened, we will annihilate them [India]."[166] However,

unbeknownst to Islamabad, Modi had already made his decision in favor of a limited military strike and conveyed it to his senior-most advisers on September 23.[167]

On September 29, Indian DGMO Singh announced that the army had carried out "surgical strikes" the night before against terrorist "launch pads" on the Pakistani side of the LOC. "Terrorist teams," he said, "had positioned themselves" at these staging areas "with an aim to carry out infiltration and terrorist strikes in Jammu and Kashmir and in various other metros in our country." Singh claimed that the Indian strikes had caused "significant casualties," but pointedly added that the army had no "plans for continuation of further operations." Lastly, Singh said that he had informed the Pakistani DGMO of the Indian operation and "explained our concerns."[168] In the following days, details of the "surgical strikes" emerged in the Indian and international media, although many of them were contradictory or simply mistaken.[169] Apparently, some 70–80 special forces commandos crossed the LOC on foot under cover of Indian mortar and machine gun fire. Armed with assault rifles, rocket-propelled grenades, shoulder-fired missiles, pistols, and plastic explosives, the soldiers advanced some 1–3 kilometers into Pakistan-administered territory and attacked six to seven launch pads—essentially safe houses where militants gather prior to infiltration across the LOC. Early Indian estimates put the number of militants killed in the raids as high as 45, which is almost certainly inflated. The *Economist*'s estimate of "a dozen or fewer" killed is probably clos-er to the mark.[170]

While some early accounts of the Indian strikes portrayed them as a fundamental change in New Delhi's policy regarding Pakistan's support for subconventional operations across the LOC,[171] it was soon revealed that In-dia had occasionally executed its own shallow incursions across the LOC to prevent and disrupt such operations.[172] What was different this time was the "public—and political" announcement of the strikes.[173] Of all the available mil-itary options, Modi had chosen the one that was least likely to escalate into a larger conflict with Pakistan,[174] while at the same time sending a message to Is-lamabad, the international community, and Modi's frenzied domestic audience. Indeed, the option he chose was so lim-ited that Pakistani leaders were able to deny that it even happened, so as to pre-empt pressures from their own public to retaliate in ways that might spark esca-lation. Pakistani officials termed India's assertion of "surgical strikes" a "fabrica-tion," claiming instead that two of their soldiers were killed by Indian forces fir-ing across the LOC.[175] New Delhi had also received diplomatic cover from the United States in the form of a telephone conversation between national security adviser Doval and his U.S. counterpart, Susan Rice. In that conversation, which seems to have occurred just before the strikes, Rice "strongly condemned" the Uri attack and highlighted the "danger that cross-border terrorism poses to the region."[176] Indian officials publicized Rice's message at the same time that the surgical strikes were announced, leaving the strong impression that Washington supported India's right to self-defense and did not oppose the attacks.

In the immediate aftermath of In-dia's surgical strikes, both sides braced themselves for more violence. Fearing a Pakistani reprisal, India ordered an evacuation of communities in a 10-ki-lometer belt along the Punjab border between the two countries.[177] New Del-hi also raised the alert status of its West-ern and Northern commands and can-celed leaves in both commands,[178] while the Pakistan Army maintained its own heightened state of readiness and also canceled all leaves.[179] Clashes continued in their "normal" fashion across the LOC, with regular exchanges of small arms and mortar fire.[180] At the same time, the two governments indicated that they did not wish to see the fighting escalate. In the first week of October, the Indian and Pakistani national security advisers spoke by phone multiple times and agreed to defuse tensions along the LOC.[181] Modi's decision to retaliate in a limited way across the LOC, targeting militants rather than Pakistan army forces, combined with Islamabad's de-cision to deny that the surgical strikes had even taken place, dampened what otherwise might have developed into a full-blown Indo-Pakistani crisis.

Comparative Analysis

This section analyzes the relative strength of the four most com-mon explanations for India's moderation in response to Pakistani and Pakistan-abetted armed provocations over the last two decades. Again, this is not a question of one explanation being "right" and the others "wrong." Monocausal explanations rarely suffice when it comes to complex national decisions regarding the use of force. Rather, a combination of three of the four factors presented in the introduction—nuclear deterrence, U.S. crisis management, and the lack of good conventional military options—more effectively explains Indian forbearance in the face of Pakistani provocations. Below, I assess their relative importance to generate a rich explanation. My analysis leads me to conclude that the *primary* factor causing India to demonstrate "uncommon restraint after severe provocations"[182] has been nuclear deterrence. Two other factors, U.S. crisis management and the absence of good conventional military options, were also influential across the four conflict episodes, but less so. The least compelling factor was the ostensible doctrine of Indian strategic restraint, which rests on shaky premises. Both secondary factors are closely tied—and subservient—to nuclear weapons, which sparked energetic U.S. crisis management efforts and severely limited Indian conventional military options. Moreover, nuclear deterrence was the real cause of India's "strategic restraint."

Each of the four cases under examination began with aggression against India emanating from Pakistan. Two of the attacks—one by Pakistani forces in 1999, the other by Pakistan-based terrorists in 2016—involved breaches of the LOC dividing the two countries' territory in Kashmir. The other two assaults were carried out in

India's largest cities—New Delhi in 2001 and Mumbai in 2008—by terrorist groups with close ties to Pakistan's intelligence agency, the ISI. (And the 2001 onslaught was followed by another mass-casualty attack against an Indian military installation in Kashmir in 2002.) Each of these strikes was severely provocative, because of the large number of fatalities, the audacity of the target, or both. In every case, India's most senior national security officials convened quickly in the CCS to discuss a range of potential responses.[183] The mooted military options tended to involve everything from very limited, post-Uri-like ground incursions across the LOC, to air strikes against terrorist targets in Pakistani Kashmir or Punjab, to a conventional ground invasion across the international border.[184] In each case, the Indian prime minister chose a measured response tailored to avoid escalation to major conventional war, and possibly a nuclear exchange.

Nuclear deterrence was the deepest root of Indian caution. Any analysis of the role of nuclear deterrence on Indian decision making must begin with a simple truth: It is difficult, if not impossible, to "prove" that nuclear deterrence "worked" in any given case. In order to do so, one would have to compile mutually consistent, authoritative accounts of key decision makers, to the effect that they were primed to order military operations but refrained from acting because they feared nuclear retaliation by the other side or an escalation spiral that might lead to a nuclear exchange. Indian leaders would naturally be reluctant to admit either that they were actively planning military strikes *or*—more importantly—that they were dissuaded from doing so by Pakistani nuclear weapons, which would signal weakness and set a bad precedent.[185] As Robert Jervis writes, "to project an image of high resolve and preserve their bargaining power for future confrontations, states have an interest in minimizing the extent to which others believe that they were influenced by their adversary's threats, especially threats to use nuclear weapons."[186] What analysts sometimes forget is that it is equally difficult to "prove" that nuclear deterrence "did not work" during a particular conflict episode. Nuclear deterrence is a psychological process wherein one side's capabilities and signaling work in often subtle ways on the perceptions, fears, and ambitions of the other side's most important actors. What we are left with, then, is to assess the *plausibility* of deterrence having "worked."

Generally speaking, the effects of nuclear deterrence on Indian behavior since 1998 have been twofold. First, the option of a major conventional military invasion of Pakistani territory (not Pakistani Kashmir) is no longer feasible for Indian decision makers. This is a stark contrast with South Asia's pre-nuclear era, when New Delhi launched substantial ground attacks on Pakistani soil during wars over Kashmir in 1965 and Bangladesh in 1971. The implications of this change can scarcely be overstated. What it means is that the punitive option that would best leverage India's overall advantages in material power over Pakistan, a war of attrition employing India's greater military and economic resources, has been removed from the Indian strategic toolkit. Second, Indian planners are acutely aware that *any* substantial military response to cross-border provocations raises the possibility of an escalation spiral that is fraught with peril and might lead to nuclear war. As a consequence, they have been forced to choose options that have little or no chance of triggering a process of escalation to conventional, and then possibly nuclear, war. Thus, India's abiding strategic dilemma in South Asia's nuclear era is that any military offensive robust enough to compel Pakistan to change its behavior runs the risk of nuclear retaliation, while Indian military strikes that are certain *not* to provoke a Pakistani nuclear response, or an escalatory spiral that might lead to such a response, are unlikely to change Pakistan's behavior.

During the 1999 Kargil crisis, India responded forcefully after the discovery of Pakistani intruders on its side of the LOC in Kashmir.[187] However, India's military forces had strict orders from the political leadership to carefully limit their operations to the *Indian* side of the LOC, despite the fact that more aggressive operations *across* the LOC would have empowered the air force and army to disrupt Pakistani supply lines and shortened the conflict. One source says that Pakistan made four distinct nuclear threats toward India in an attempt to deter New Delhi from escalating the conflict.[188] Moreover, each side repositioned its ballistic missiles, raising concerns across the border. These signals seem to have worked: numerous analysts "concur that the prospect of a Pakistani nuclear reprisal deterred New Delhi from escalating the conflict in ways that not only would have worked to India's tactical advantage, but also would have saved Indian lives."[189] Paul Kapur marshals an impressive roster of senior Indian officials who deny that Pakistan's nuclear weapons deterred Indian forces from breaching the LOC in 1999.[190] But, other accounts suggest that some of those same Indian leaders were actually very mindful of the nuclear dangers. One observes that "Prime Minister Vajpayee was known to have seriously considered a Pakistani nuclear strike had India escalated the war." In a "crucial closed-door meeting, ... Vajpayee expressed his apprehension about Pakistan using the nuclear weapon if India enlarged the conflict by crossing the LOC."[191] Army chief Malik recounts that "the nuclear weapons factor played on the minds of the political decision makers ... political and military planning and preparation for conflict escalation had to be carried out carefully. Escalation control was essential."[192] It was not the fear of an immediate Pakistani nuclear reprisal that deterred New Delhi from sending its army across the LOC; it was, rather, Indian officials' understanding that the war could escalate from there to the international border, and perhaps beyond, into the nuclear realm. Many observers have pointed out that this dynamic represents a distinct shift in Indian behavior since the 1965 war, which began with a clandestine Pakistani effort to foment rebellion among Muslims in Indian Kashmir. For example, Narang writes that: "The BJP, fearing Pakistan's

now-credible nuclear threats, curtailed the Indian military's options to expel Pakistani forces and strictly prevented any operations on or above Pakistani soil. This was in striking contrast to the manner in which India had conducted previous engagements with Pakistan, most notably in response to the 1965 infiltration, which provided the blueprint for Kargil."[193] Although Indian officials are circumspect about admitting that they were deterred by Pakistan from choosing more muscular military options, for the reasons noted above, "it is exceedingly difficult to imagine their having been so restrained in the absence of the dissuasive power of Pakistan's nuclear weapons. This is especially so when 1999 is viewed in contrast to the 1965 Indo-Pakistani war, when—in response to successive Pakistani provocations—India chose escalatory options both in disputed Kashmir *and* along the international border."[194]

The influence of nuclear deterrence on Indian calculations during the 2001–02 crisis was even more profound. For nine months after the attack on the Parliament complex, India and Pakistan's armed forces were mobilized along the international border and LOC, including long stretches of time at their highest alert levels. India enjoyed an advantage with three strike corps to Pakistan's two; unlike during Kargil, the Indian strike corps were poised for action in their forward launch areas. Both sides tested nuclear-capable ballistic missiles and repositioned missiles closer to the international border. Pakistan also deployed its nuclear-capable attack aircraft to forward bases near the border.[195] Senior officials on both sides exchanged pointed, aggressive, nuclear-tinged threats. Pakistani president Musharraf recollects that he transmitted repeated nuclear-deterrent messages to Indian prime minister Vajpayee via intermediaries. One retrospective analysis counted 17 nuclear threats, nine issued by Pakistan and eight by India.[196] India was ready to launch major conventional military operations, and Vajpayee apparently came very close to making a decision for war in both January and June 2002.[197]

Instead, he chose peace. Authoritative accounts based on extensive interviews point to nuclear deterrence as the main factor inducing New Delhi to stand down. "The risk of nuclear escalation, [Indian] officials said, was important in shaping Indian policy responses. Vajpayee feared that a full-scale military response to Pakistan-backed terrorism could precipitate a wider conflagration." Even small reprisals across the LOC could lead to an escalatory spiral—a "possibility unacceptable in a nuclear South Asia." The same source concludes that "nuclear weapons played a central role in ensuring that the crisis provoked by the terror strike on India's Parliament did not lead to war."[198] Vajpayee's National Security Adviser, Brajesh Mishra, recollects that in January 2002 there "was a 90 per cent possibility of going to war."[199] Mishra says: "we were pretty sure—fairly certain—that if we crossed the border, Pakistan would threaten the use of nuclear weapons. Actual use is uncertain, perhaps doubtful." In Mishra's view, "the risk of nuclear weapons use increased sharply

as soon as Indian forces crossed either the LOC ... or more critically the international border." He maintains that "there was no such thing as limited war in the India–Pakistan context, arguing that 'if you cross the [LOC] or the Punjab border there is bound to be an all-out war,' and that Pakistan would escalate and this would be the mechanism for nuclear use."[200] Narang writes: "Just as in Kargil, India was—at great cost— deterred from employing limited, let alone overwhelming, conventional force against Pakistan across the international border or the LOC. Although several factors may have stopped Delhi from executing Parakram, the role of Pakistan's asymmetric escalation posture in deterring India's conventional assault was crucial .... Such an attack, as was contemplated in May and June 2002, risked triggering nuclear use and was thus no longer possible."[201] Indian fears were shared across the border. In interviews, President Musharraf has recalled "many sleepless nights" just after the Parliament attack, asking himself whether he would or could deploy nuclear weapons." He "contemplated the use of nuclear weapons, but decided against doing so out of fear of retaliation."[202] During the second peak of the crisis, Musharraf remembers that he "hardly slept for several nights" and "feared nuclear war." According to Michael Cohen, who interviewed Musharraf," the latter "knew that any Indian invasion would have quickly triggered Pakistani nuclear escalation," and he "worried that nuclear war would engulf his country."[203] In sum, the Twin Peaks crisis had the effect of further embedding the fear of nuclear war in the perceptions of Indian and Pakistani officials. As one analysis notes, with each new crisis, the "constraining role of nuclear weapons" became "more explicit."[204]

Despite the severity of the Mumbai attacks, the near-crisis that followed receives less attention than Kargil or Twin Peaks. This is ironic, because while this episode was relatively muted, it was muted mainly because—10 years after South Asia's overt nuclear weaponization and seven years after India's frustrating Operation Parakram—it had been established that a significant conventional Indian military response was simply out of the question. Thus, the case in which the impact of nuclear deterrence on Indian behavior may have been greatest is the least examined one. Indians were naturally outraged at the slaughter in Mumbai, but Congress Prime Minister Singh decided virtually immediately that his government would react with restraint and deliberation, not repeating the Twin Peaks rush to mobilization, which had cost India dearly in blood, treasure, and reputation. New Delhi's circumscribed response represented the evolutionary "locking in" of nuclear deterrence between the two South Asian rivals.

When Indian national security officials met after Mumbai, they discussed military options ranging from, at the high end, limited ground strikes across the Punjab border and, at the low end, "surgical strikes" against terrorist targets in Pakistani Kashmir. In between were air and/or missile strikes against terrorist "infrastructure" across the LOC, but military leaders admitted that they lacked reliable enough intelligence to recommend such operations. The strong consensus among the services was that Pakistan would retaliate for any Indian aggression, and the service chiefs made it abundantly clear that they were not ready to engage in a substantial conventional conflict with Pakistan (which will be further addressed below). Political leaders were themselves very mindful of the escalation risks, and did not want to run the risk of a nuclear exchange. Although insisting that all options were on the table, the government "conceded that its military options to retaliate against Pakistan were again limited, because any meaningful strikes risked uncontrollable escalation, possibly up to the nuclear level. India was once again deterred by Pakistan's perceived low nuclear threshold from executing retaliatory airstrikes against suspected [LeT] camps in Pakistan for fear of escalation to general war."[205] Michael Krepon writes: "[Prime Minister] Singh, like Vajpayee, appears to have concluded soon after the Mumbai attacks that the benefits of punishing Pakistan would likely be modest and the risks would likely be great. Foremost among those risks was the possibility of uncontrolled escalation resulting in nuclear detonations."[206] Because of New Delhi's subdued reaction, the resulting tension saw limited escalation and only three nuclear threats.[207] The Pakistan Army took several precautionary steps, such as moving a modest number of ground forces and heightening the alert status of others. Both air forces were briefly on alert, and the PAF carried out and loudly advertised exercises of its fighter aircraft. Ultimately, though, India refrained from launching military strikes, again demonstrating its dilemma in South Asia's overt nuclear era: meaningful military operations against Pakistan run the risk of catastrophe, while lesser ones have little chance of bringing about desired changes in Pakistani policies.

The September 2016 Uri attack and India's response again demonstrated the effects of nuclear deterrence on Indian decision making. Prime Minister Modi had repeatedly criticized New Delhi's weakness in not standing up to Pakistani provocations, often calling out his predecessor, Manmohan Singh, by name for not retaliating against Pakistan after the 2008 Mumbai slaughter. Modi's senior national security aides had pledged on many occasions that Indians could expect him to respond to Pakistani aggression with much greater resolve than had his predecessors. Then the gruesome Uri attack sparked the onset of a familiar cycle—full-throated calls for revenge in the Indian media, a cross-border war of words including a very precise nuclear threat by the Pakistani defense minister, both armies put on alert in Punjab and Kashmir, an emphatic show of force during PAF "exercises," and India's evacuation of border villages in Punjab. After the usual Indian discussion of military options, Modi then picked one with little potential for escalation to a conventional war and, possibly, a nuclear exchange. As a longtime Indian defense journalist put it, Modi "chose the option that was

least likely to escalate to an all-out war." More robust choices "were ruled out as they raised the specter of a nuclear conflict."[208]

Overall, after 20 years of an overtly nuclear South Asia, there is a broad consensus that Indian and Pakistani nuclear weapons deter major war between New Delhi and Islamabad. Stephen Cohen calls this the "reality of [nuclear] deterrence" on the Subcontinent. Ashley Tellis writes: "Pakistan's construction of a large, diversified, and ever-expanding nuclear arsenal ... serves to prevent any significant Indian retaliation against Pakistan's persistent low-intensity war for fear of sparking a nuclear holocaust." This represents an "insidious kind of 'ugly stability' over the past few decades." After the 2008 Mumbai episode, Kenneth Waltz wrote: "Both countries know that a serious conventional conflict risks a resort to nuclear weapons. Given that neither India nor Pakistan can know whether its opponent will resort to nuclear use, either inadvertently or on purpose, both are disincentivized from beginning a conventional conflict at all as the anticipated result is simply disastrous." Also after Mumbai, Krepon wrote: "Nuclear weapons have played a significant part in previous crises on the subcontinent. As deterrence optimists argue, nuclear weapons may well have reinforced caution and helped to forestall escalation across the nuclear threshold." For Narang, the Kargil, Twin Peaks, and Mumbai episodes "reveal that Pakistan's asymmetric escalation posture means that major conventional war—even in retaliation—is no longer a viable option for India ... Pakistan's ... posture inhibited Indian leaders from executing militarily effective retaliatory options that might have otherwise been on the list of choices for fear of triggering Pakistani nuclear use." In George Perkovich's view, expressed just after the Uri attack, "mutual nuclear deterrence has made leaders on both sides conclude that major warfare between the two states would be suicidal." But, the Pakistan-generated "low-intensity conflict can escalate," leading to what he calls an "unstable equilibrium." The bottom line, however, is that: "The leaders of India and Pakistan understand that they have more to lose than to gain by military conflict. They both have interests in avoiding escalation, in part due to the shadow of potential nuclear war if escalation did occur." Perkovich and Toby Dalton write: "Reviewing the record of conflicts and crises in South Asia since 1990 through a prism of escalation dominance indicates that the threat of any conflict becoming nuclear has had a dampening effect on Indian strategy and decisionmaking ... The possibility of escalation drove India to limit the geographic scope of its airstrikes during the 1999 Kargil crisis. It was also a major element of the decision calculus that led India to mobilize forces but not cross the border during the 2001–2002 crisis, and to limit responses to economic and diplomatic means following the attacks in Mumbai in 2008." Rajesh Rajagopalan observes that the "fear of nuclear escalation prevented India from responding to terror attacks on ... the Indian Parliament [2001], on Indian military establishments, and on Mumbai, as well as many other less serious attacks."[209]

Another significant factor in New Delhi's choices to respond to Pakistani aggression in ways that would not escalate out of control was the crisis management role of the United States. U.S. initiatives to dissuade Indian decision makers from carrying out more punishing military operations were most important during the Kargil and Twin Peaks episodes. In the aftermath of the Mumbai attacks, U.S. intervention was significant, but less so than in 1999 and 2001–02, mainly because Prime Minister Singh decided very early on that India would not mobilize its armed forces, which in turn sent a strong signal to Pakistan and the world that New Delhi would not mount a robust military reprisal. U.S. crisis management was notably less pronounced during the 2016 Uri aftermath, with senior Obama administration officials seeming implicitly to condone India's right to respond proportionately.[210]

If it is difficult to show that nuclear deterrence has "worked" in a given situation, it is too *easy* to show that U.S. suasion "worked" in the same context. While deterrence is invisible and plausibly deniable by the deterree, crisis intervention is typically highly visible, with senior U.S. officials embarking on whirlwind tours of South Asia at critical junctures, activity that is highly visible via the media and for which the intervening government is always willing to take credit. Particularly salient in this regard were trips to the region by CENTCOM commander Zinni in June

1999, as the Indian government was facing severe escalatory pressures during the Kargil conflict; by Deputy Secretary of State Armitage in June 2002, as the Twin Peaks crisis crested its second peak; and by Secretary of State Rice and JCS chairman Mullen during the Mumbai tensions in December 2008. Furthermore, in all three cases, presidents Clinton and Bush energetically worked the phones with their Indian and Pakistani interlocutors.

Just as important as the fact, and number, of the visits and phone calls by U.S. (and occasionally British) officials was the message they consistently hammered home; namely, that any escalation of the crises to substantial cross-border military operations would run a serious risk of further tit-for-tat escalation. Were that to happen, U.S. leaders could easily imagine two possible paths to a nuclear exchange: first, if India decided during such an escalation process to invade Pakistan, and its forces were winning preliminary engagements and making progress into Punjab or Sindh, Islamabad would begin to consider, and perhaps eventually order, nuclear strikes against the invading forces or on targets within India; second, the fog of war during escalation would generate severe stresses on men and machines, with the possibility of inadvertent escalation to a nuclear exchange growing with every step up the ladder. In each case except for Uri in 2016, there was a distinct synergy between nuclear deterrence and U.S. conflict management, which complemented, reinforced, and strengthened each other. However, nuclear deterrence

deserves pride of place, because if nuclear weapons had not been potentially involved, crisis-management efforts would have been less urgent, possibly even negligible. This synergy between them was demonstrated most obviously during the Kargil conflict, whose denouement included the extraordinary meeting in which President Clinton accused Pakistan of "messing with nuclear war." Zinni, too, was unsparing in his language to Pakistani officials: "I put forward a simple rationale for withdrawing: 'If you don't pull back, you're going to bring war and nuclear annihilation down on your country.'"[211] As Lavoy summarizes the synergy between nuclear deterrence and crisis management in 1999, "the fear of nuclear war did drive the international community to end the crisis as quickly as possible and prevent Pakistan from claiming a victory that could validate a defense strategy based on nuclear threats and military aggression."[212] Similar dynamics were apparent in the Twin Peaks and Mumbai cases. U.S. diplomatic intervention undoubtedly played a role in persuading Indian leaders not to attack Pakistan in response to the terrorist attacks in New Delhi, Kashmir, and Mumbai. Here again, though, it is virtually impossible to disentangle U.S. diplomacy from the underlying fear of possible escalation to a nuclear exchange. As Krepon writes, "Washington did not need much prompting to engage in crisis management, as nuclear capabilities and the potential for missteps, accidents, and breakdowns in command and control grew on the subcontinent. While nuclear dangers during crises remained hard to assess, underestimating them was a luxury that senior US policy makers could not afford."[213]

One analysis completely discounts the role of nuclear weapons and deterrence in arguing that U.S. conflict management was the cause of Indian restraint during Kargil and Twin Peaks. Mistry maintains that these "crises ended because of non-nuclear factors rather than because of nuclear deterrence. A larger war was averted not because—as supporters of nuclear deterrence theory would suggest—the threat of Pakistani nuclear retaliation deterred Indian military action against Pakistan. Instead, war was averted because of U.S. diplomatic efforts that restrained the parties from military escalation."[214] It is difficult to accept the idea that, in two major crises within four years of India and Pakistan conclusively demonstrating their long extant nuclear prowess, nuclear weapons would have had no discernible effect at all on the perceptions and strategic calculations of Indian decision makers. Part of the problem with Mistry's analysis is that he repeatedly conflates Indian planning that was not deterred and escalatory possibilities with actual military operations. His article is littered with Indian military actions that "could have" happened, "would have" happened, were "likely to have" happened, "came close" to happening, and other similar formulations.[215] At one point, he writes about the Twin Peaks crisis: "Neither was India's military deterred from an attack against Pakistan. India's military came close to attacking Pakistan on two occasions."[216] (Emphasis added.) Surely attacks either happen

or they do not, and nuclear deterrence is about deterring action rather than planning. In any event, Mistry contradicts himself by offering a more tenable posture in another 2009 writing: "The [Kargil and Twin Peaks] crises did not escalate to a major war. Nuclear deterrence induced caution among security planners on both sides and was one factor that checked them from quickly escalating to large-scale military operations, although conventional deterrence and international diplomacy also contributed to this military restraint."[217] The threat of escalation to the nuclear level provided both the best reason for Washington's crisis management efforts and the most compelling argument U.S. interlocutors could use to ease the two sides away from war.

A third causal factor in the pattern of Indian moderation has been New Delhi's lack of favorable conventional military options at key moments. This might be framed as conventional deterrence, but—here again—it is analytically difficult to disentangle conventional from nuclear inhibitions against the Indian use of large-scale force. As noted previously, Pakistan's nuclear weapons have taken away the option that in South Asia's pre-nuclear era was India's ace in the hole: a major conventional assault across the India–Pakistan frontier that would take advantage of India's superiority in armored strike forces, attack aircraft, and overall material resources to overwhelm Pakistan's armed forces.[218] For the last two decades, India's conventional military advantage has rested not on glaring net asymmetries between Indian and Pakistani air and ground forces,[219] but rather in its ability to grind Pakistan down in a longer, attrition-style ground war. But, this is exactly the type of assault Pakistan's nuclear weapons and asymmetric escalation posture most credibly deter.[220] During the cases under examination, if India had clear, even blitzkrieg-level, superiority in ground forces, and could have inflicted a severe defeat on Pakistani forces, it would have run serious risks of a nuclear reprisal. Furthermore, looming over Indian consideration of even limited conventional strikes across the established international border is that India is damned if it loses, but also damned if it wins, because Pakistan might well respond to imminent defeat by resorting to nuclear weapons. Large military organizations are not enthusiastic about, or good at, winning big ... but not too big. The champions of Cold Start-type limited war operations have not succeeded in convincing their political masters that they know where the line is between penetrating "far enough" versus "too far" into a nuclearized Pakistan.

Even absent the constraints imposed on Indian decision making by Pakistan's nuclear weapons, it is arguably the case that India has never had good options for going on the offensive against Pakistan over the last 20 years. Strikes against terrorist targets across the LOC are likely to have minimal impact on Pakistan's willingness to support cross-LOC attacks. Kashmir's mountainous terrain is unpromising for meaningful conventional incursions, militants are likely to have evacuated their rudimentary encampments

and escaped at first warning of major Indian military operations, and—in any event—Pakistan's terrorist infrastructure extends well beyond Kashmir. Only a successful Indian conventional invasion across the international border might compel changes in Pakistani behavior, but—nuclear weapons aside—analysts tend to agree that India does not have sufficient conventional superiority along its Western frontier to be confident of victory. India's overall advantages in conventional military forces are reduced by its need to keep hundreds of thousands of troops engaged in Kashmir[221] and deployed in the eastern part of the country against potential threats from China. Although the Indian army has three strike corps to Pakistan's two, their peacetime positions are relatively far from the border, and their mobilization times remain slow. Pakistan Army strike corps are much closer to the border in peacetime, and the country's narrow geography means that its internal lines of supply and communications are considerably shorter than its opponent's. Because India would be unlikely to have the advantage of strategic surprise in a sudden crisis, by the time its strike corps are poised for battle after 2–3 weeks of mobilization, Pakistan's would be well positioned for both defensive and counter-offensive operations.[222] While India enjoys somewhat favorable ratios of tanks, fighter aircraft, and other equipment, these ratios are not high enough for Indian military planners to provide assurances of success to the political leadership.[223] Lastly, India's armed forces have been plagued by obsolete tanks, armored vehicles, artillery pieces, and other equipment, as well as chronic shortages of officers, ammunition, missiles, air defense assets, and war stores.[224]

These restraints on India's conventional warfighting potential came into play in each of the four cases. During Kargil and Twin Peaks, official Indian estimates put the country's conventional combat edge over Pakistan at an estimated 1.1–1.2:1, essentially "operational-level parity."[225] The official Indian government review of the Kargil conflict says flatly: "On the Indian side, it had been made abundantly clear that the Indian Army has not for sometime enjoyed a punitive edge over the Pakistan Army to adopt an effective pro-active strategy"[226] were India to escalate the fighting. During Twin Peaks, New Delhi opted for a full mobilization of Indian forces without any specific guidance as to what their mission(s) would be. V.K. Singh, then a Brigadier with the XI Corps in Punjab, recalls that the "very first few days of Operation Parakram exposed the hollowness of our operational preparedness."[227] With three strike corps ready to roll out of their launch areas, Prime Minister Vajpayee twice backed away from the brink of war. One account quotes a senior BJP foreign policy adviser as saying, "'the notion that international pressure from the United States impelled India to hold fire in 2001–2002 and defuse the crisis was a political excuse. The real problem was a lack of viable military options.'"[228] In 2008, Prime Minister Singh, apparently having learned from the 2002 mobilization fiasco, resisted pressures to order the

Indian military into action in retaliation for the Mumbai massacre. Singh's instinctive caution was undoubtedly bolstered by senior army leaders' view that an "inadequate and obsolete arsenal at their disposal mitigated against" war.[229] The army chief's admission that India was unprepared for war with Pakistan was the "most visible manifestation of the 'hollowing out' of the Indian Army."[230] After intensive discussion of options, even the most limited military response was ruled out, owing partly to Indian conventional deficiencies.[231] In 2016, with Indian military forces still suffering from shortcomings that "raise serious questions whether India can undertake large-scale military operations at all," and which suggest that "Indian policy makers cannot be confident that even a limited resort to military force would achieve a rapid result,"[232] Prime Minister Modi belied his more hawkish reputation by ordering pinprick military operations in Kashmir that were militarily insignificant. One influential Indian defense analyst was of the view that Indian conventional warfighting capabilities were even worse in 2016 than they had been in 2008.[233]

A fourth potential explanation for Indian forbearance in the face of repeated provocations is New Delhi's alleged "strategic restraint doctrine," which is said to be a driving force behind the political leadership's tight limitations on the use of military force.[234] For Cohen and Dasgupta, India has a "deeply embedded tradition of strategic restraint." In this view, "reticence in the use of force as an instrument of state policy has been the dominant political condition for Indian thinking on the military."[235] This "long-standing international political–military posture" can be traced to the views of Indian nationalist heroes like Gandhi and Nehru, who "saw the use of armed force as normatively flawed and practically costly for India." Going back to Independence, this argument continues, "the Indian political leadership has generally seen military force as an inappropriate instrument of politics."[236] Indian strategic restraint is rooted in a "political culture stressing disengagement, avoidance of confrontation, and a defensive mindset."[237] In Sarang Shidore's conception, strategic restraint is one of the "operational elements" of India's strategic culture specifically "with respect to nuclear weapons and security relations with Pakistan." Shidore traces India's alleged strategic restraint to the post-Independence leadership: "Moralism has traditionally been a prominent driver in India's strategic restraint doctrine. Nehruvian ideas of resolution of conflict through communication influenced the defining of Indian restraint."[238] In more recent decades, he says, "liberal globalism is also a driver for the continued persistence of India's strategic restraint policy"; New Delhi's economic liberalization and high economic growth rates have generated a "view that a major conflict with Pakistan carries unacceptable risks to India's prospects for development and security."[239] One proponent of this argument, retired Indian brigadier Gurmeet Kanwal, claims that New Delhi has observed "immense strategic restraint" in the face of "grave provocation." As examples, he includes: "low-intensity limited conflict and proxy war since 1947 in Jammu and Kashmir; Pakistan's Operation Gibraltar (1965); Pakistani support to the Khalistan movement in Indian Punjab (1980s); the Kargil conflict (1999); the attack on the Indian parliament, Operation Parakram, and the attack on Indian Army family quarters, Kaluchak (2001–02); and the Mumbai terrorist strikes (2008).[240] Shidore concurs, writing that "strategic restraint in Indian security policy is largely borne out by the empirical record with respect to Pakistan. India's response to pointed provocations such as terrorist attacks has traditionally been overwhelmingly diplomatic rather than military." He specifically refers to Kargil, Twin Peaks, and Mumbai as good examples of Indian strategic restraint in practice.[241]

Although a comprehensive history of India's use of military force is beyond the scope of this article, there are strong reasons to doubt that a doctrine of strategic restraint has caused India to shy away from wielding military power, either in general or during the episodes examined above. In the pre-nuclear era, New Delhi ordered substantial military operations in Kashmir in the autumn of 1947, a provocative and disastrous "forward policy" toward China in the leadup to the Sino–Indian war of 1962, an invasion across the international border with Pakistan in 1965 (escalating the second Kashmir war, begun by Pakistan), another invasion of Pakistan during the Bangladesh war of 1971, a military occupation of the Siachen Glacier in 1984, and an enormous military exercise in Punjab which kicked off the Brasstacks crisis and near-war with Pakistan in 1986–87. Drawing on Alastair Iain Johnston's theoretical framework,[242] Ali Ahmed argues convincingly that "India has not shied away from the use of force. Such resort has been discreet and conditioned by strategic considerations. It has displayed both resolve and restraint." Furthermore, the "operational set in India's strategic culture was never as pacifist as suggested by India's popular self-image."[243]

In the post-nuclear era, India has mounted vigorous attacks against Pakistani positions during the Kargil conflict,[244] attempted via a massive military mobilization in 2001–02 to coerce Pakistan to modify its behavior,[245] and resorted to "surgical strikes" across the LOC on several occasions, including after the 2016 Uri massacre. However, unlike in the pre-nuclear era, New Delhi has refrained from launching major attacks across the LOC or the international border. As discussed in previous sections, the combined effects of nuclear deterrence, U.S. crisis management, and a dearth of good conventional military options together provide a robust explanation for Indian restraint. Nuclear weapons, in particular, have induced demonstrable caution, evident in the cases presented above and in the numerous scholarly analyses cited in this article. In contrast, supporters of the strategic restraint explanation never even attempt to show through evidence or a specific causal mechanism that such a "doctrine" in fact animates Indian behavior. Their ar-

gument is tautological: India acts with restraint; therefore, it must have a doctrine of strategic restraint. Indeed, they sometimes inadvertently betray their belief that the *primary* phenomenon at play is actually nuclear deterrence, while strategic restraint is distinctly *epiphenomenal*. For example, Dasgupta and Cohen maintain that "once India and Pakistan accepted the basic reality of nuclear deterrence ... restraint by choice became restraint without choice. No Indian leader could risk the chance of a Pakistani [nuclear] attack on an Indian city."[246] Cohen, writing with two colleagues about Kargil, notes that Indian "restraint was in marked contrast to India's response in the 1965 and 1971 conflicts, when nuclear weapons had not entered the equation and it had not displayed any inhibitions in invading Pakistan."[247] Another observer writes about Twin Peaks: "Vajpayee's admirers would praise him for 'strategic restraint.' His critics called him indecisive. No one, in public at least, would admit the possibility that he might be being realistic. The Indian Army was not in a position to deal a decisive blow against Pakistan."[248] Strategic restraint in its truest sense is simply an inclination toward moderation under the nuclear shadow. "It means responding in a way that does not potentially become strategically costly for India by risking a broader conventional war, which carries with it not only human and economic costs, but also the risk of nuclear use if the war spills across the international border."[249] Claiming a doctrine of "strategic restraint" makes a virtue out of necessity.

Implications

The main causes of Indian temperance in the four cases examined in this paper are nuclear deterrence, a paucity of good conventional military options, and U.S. efforts to manage Indo-Pakistani conflicts, and ease tensions. Nuclear deterrence is the most significant of these factors, because it spawns and strengthens the other two. The underlying presence of nuclear weapons triggers U.S. conflict management and provides the most compelling rationale for Indian and Pakistani interlocutors to heed the warnings of U.S. diplomats. The ever-present possibility of escalation to the use of nuclear weapons strictly limits Indian conventional military options, including the one most likely to inflict defeat on Pakistani forces and potentially bring an end to Islamabad's subconventional operations on Indian soil (including Indian Kashmir). Framed another way, nuclear deterrence is the cause which, if taken away, would make the most difference. It is difficult to imagine that the Indian political leadership would, in the absence of nuclear weapons, have resisted pressures to order more punitive military strikes against Pakistan.

Given the daunting constraints they have faced when contemplating the retaliatory use of force against Pakistan, Indian decision makers have acted with prudence, wisdom, and rationality. Unfortunately, this is not how many Indians see it. Indian analysts and the population at large, justifiably livid after years of Pakistani and Pakistan-supported attacks, often bemoan their political leaders' lack of "resolve" in not responding with decisive military force. While their frustration is understandable, they should instead celebrate their government's sober assessments of the costs and benefits of striking back hard against Pakistan. Indian decision making is the chief firebreak against major, possibly nuclear, war in South Asia. Indians should prefer that the power of escalation control rest in their hands, rather than in Pakistan's. Crossing the international border with large conventional military forces has now been established as the brightest of red lines in a nuclear South Asia. Like early American nuclear analysts before them, Indian strategists are chafing against the dictates of the nuclear revolution. They continue to search desperately for "space" under the nuclear threshold to punish Pakistan for its transgressions, coming up with a range of Cold-Start-type "proactive" options. But, the political leadership is rightly skeptical of these "solutions," instinctively understanding that there really is no safe "space" for substantial conventional operations, given the never-negligible chance that armed clashes might escalate out of control. Two analysts capture the essential logic of Indian restraint: "as horrific as these acts [against India] are … they are not existential threats to Indian security—but overreaction and a war that risks nuclear escalation could be."[250] Hard as it is to stomach, India's strategic elites should accept, not resist, the simple logic of the nuclear revolution.

The first priority of any two adversarial nuclear weapon states should be to establish and institutionalize a relationship of mutual nuclear deterrence. Unfortunately, Pakistan is likely to keep poking and prodding, testing India and attempting to keep Kashmir on the boil. Indian political leaders should continue to resist pressures from the armed forces, domestic political opponents, the 24/7 media, and the public to rise to Pakistan's bait by retaliating with sizable conventional military attacks. Indian strategists should also abandon their hopeless quest for Cold Start-style limited war options under the nuclear threshold.[251] Continuing to design and publicly discuss "limited" invasion plans that, if implemented, might spark a Pakistani nuclear riposte is simply unwise. There is no prospect that Indian military planners can, in the abstract, calculate the precise magnitude of a limited conventional attack that is appropriately punitive, effective in coerc-

ing Islamabad to revise its strategy of subconventional provocations, but not so threatening to Pakistan's vital interests that it would not unleash its nuclear arsenal in response. India's "Cold Start" discourse plays directly into the hands of the Pakistan Army, which has used it to build its case for the deployment of tactical nuclear weapons and what it calls "full-spectrum deterrence." Furthermore, were Indian leaders actually to yield to the temptation of launching a "limited" military offensive, Pakistanis would rally around the flag, reinforcing the Pakistan Army's dominant position in society. At the same time, Pakistan-based terrorists would not be put out of business; indeed, a major India–Pakistan war is high on their list of goals. In short, under the nuclear shadow, any movement up the escalation ladder is potentially catastrophic.

Notes

1   I use this terminology instead of the word "crises," because the 2008 and 2016 cases were arguably not actual crises. For a contrary view, see Sameer Lalwani and Hannah Haegeland, eds., *Investigating Crises: South Asia's Lessons, Evolving Dynamics, and Trajectories* (Washington, DC: Stimson Center, 2018).

2   For an overview, see Sumit Ganguly, *Deadly Impasse: Indo-Pakistani Relations at the Dawn of a New Century* (Cambridge: Cambridge University Press, 2016). I will refer to the disputed territory in the conventional shorthand, as "Kashmir." While each side claims the entirety of Kashmir, the Indian- and Pakistani-administered parts of the territory have been divided by a line of control (LOC) since the 1972 Simla Agreement. For the sake of convenience, I refer to these areas as "Indian Kashmir" and "Pakistani Kashmir."

3   Detailed accounts of the Kargil conflict include: Sumit Ganguly and Devin T. Hagerty, *Fearful Symmetry: India–Pakistan Crises in the Shadow of Nuclear Weapons* (Seattle: University of Washington Press, 2005), 143-66; Government of India, *From Surprise to Reckoning: The Kargil Review Committee Report* (New Delhi: Sage, 2000); S. Paul Kapur, *Dangerous Deterrent: Nuclear Weapons Proliferation and Conflict in South Asia* (Stanford, CA: Stanford University Press, 2007), 117-31; Peter R. Lavoy, ed., *Asymmetric Warfare in South Asia: The Causes and Consequences of the Kargil Conflict* (New York: Cambridge University Press, 2009); V.P. Malik, *Kargil: From Surprise to Victory* (New Delhi: HarperCollins, 2006); Pervez Musharraf, *In the*

Line of Fire: A Memoir (New York: Free Press, 2006), 87-98; Shaukat Qadir, "An Analysis of the Kargil Conflict 1999," *RUSI Journal*, 147, no. 2 (April 2002): 24-30; Praveen Swami, *The Kargil War* (New Delhi: LeftWord, 2000); and Ashley J. Tellis, C. Christine Fair, and Jamison Jo Medby, *Limited Conflicts under the Nuclear Umbrella: Indian and Pakistani Lessons from the Kargil Crisis* (Santa Monica, CA: Rand, 2001).

4   On Pakistan's support for JeM and other terrorist groups, see S. Paul Kapur, *Jihad as Grand Strategy: Islamist Militancy, National Security, and the Pakistani State* (New York: Oxford University Press, 2017).

5   In-depth studies of the Twin Peaks crisis include: P.R. Chari, Pervaiz Iqbal Cheema, and Stephen P. Cohen, *Four Crises and a Peace Process: American Engagement in South Asia* (Washington, DC: Brookings, 2007), 149-83; Ganguly and Hagerty, *Fearful Symmetry*, 167-86; Kapur, *Dangerous Deterrent*, 131-39; Polly Nayak and Michael Krepon, "U.S. Crisis Management in South Asia's Twin Peaks Crisis," Report 57, The Stimson Center, Washington, DC, September 2006; and V.K. Sood and Pravin Sawhney, *Operation Parakram: The War Unfinished* (New Delhi: Sage, 2003).

6   On LeT and its connections to the Pakistani state, see Stephen Tankel, *Storming the World Stage: The Story of Lashkar-e-Taiba* (New York: Columbia University Press, 2011).

7   Detailed accounts of the 2008 Mumbai attacks include: Myra MacDonald, *Defeat Is an Orphan: How Pakistan Lost the Great South Asian War* (London: Hurst, 2017), 189-207; Shivshankar Menon, *Choices: Inside the Making of India's Foreign Policy* (Washington, DC: Brookings, 2016), 60-81; Polly Nayak and Michael Krepon, *The Unfinished Crisis: U.S. Crisis Management after the 2008 Mumbai Attacks* (Washington, DC: Stimson Center, 2012); Bruce Riedel, *Avoiding Armageddon: America, India, and Pakistan to the Brink and Back* (Washington, DC: Brookings, 2013), 1-25; Cathy Scott-Clark and Adrian Levy, *The Siege: 68 Hours Inside the Taj Hotel* (New York: Penguin, 2013); and Tankel, *Storming the World Stage*, 207-33.

8   For overviews of the Uri attack and Indian response, see Arka Biswas, "Surgical Strikes and Deterrence-Stability in South Asia," *ORF Occasional Paper No. 115* (Observer Research Foundation, New Delhi, June 2017); Nitin A. Gokhale, *Securing India the Modi Way: Pathankot, Surgical Strikes and More* (New Delhi: Bloomsbury, 2017), 1-52; Lalwani and Haegeland, eds., *Investigating Crises*; MacDonald, *Defeat Is an Orphan*, 255-61.

9   Representative treatments include: Sumit Ganguly in Sumit Ganguly and S. Paul Kapur, *India, Pakistan, and the Bomb: Debating Nuclear Stability in South Asia* (New York: Columbia University Press, 2010); Ganguly and Hagerty, *Fearful Symmetry*; Vipin Narang, *Nuclear Strategy in the Modern Era: Regional Powers and International Conflict* (Princeton, NJ: Princeton University Press, 2014), 253-82; and Kenneth Waltz in Scott D. Sagan and Kenneth N. Waltz, *The Spread of Nuclear Weapons: An Enduring Debate*, 3rd ed. (New York: W.W. Norton, 2013).

10   See Dinshaw Mistry, "Tempering Optimism about Nuclear Deterrence in South Asia," *Security Studies* 18, no. 1 (2009): 148-82; Nayak and Krepon, "U.S. Crisis Management"; Nayak and Krepon, *Unfinished Crisis*; Moeed Yusuf, *Brokering Peace in Nuclear Environments: U.S. Crisis Management in South Asia* (Stanford, CA: Stanford University Press, 2018); and Moeed Yusuf and Jason A. Kirk, "Keeping an Eye on South Asian Skies: America's Pivotal Deterrence in Nuclearized India–Pakistan Crises," *Contemporary Security Policy* 37, no. 2 (May 2016): 246-72.

11   Works in this vein include: Stephen P. Cohen and Sunil Dasgupta, *Arming without Aiming: India's Military Modernization* (Washington, DC: Brookings, 2010); Sunil Dasgupta and

Stephen P. Cohen, "Is India Ending Its Strategic Restraint Doctrine?" *Washington Quarterly* 34, no. 2 (Spring 2011): 163-77; and Sarang Shidore, "India's Strategic Culture and Deterrence Stability on the Subcontinent," in *Deterrence Instability and Nuclear Weapons in South Asia*, ed. Michael Krepon et al. (Washington, DC: Stimson Center, 2015), 119-47.

12 For works focused on the India–Pakistan conventional military balance, see: Christopher Clary, "Deterrence Stability and the Conventional Balance of Forces in South Asia," in *Deterrence Stability and Escalation Control in South Asia*, ed. Michael Krepon and Julia Thompson (Washington, DC: Stimson Center, 2012), 135-60, and Walter Ladwig, III, "Indian Military Modernization and Conventional Deterrence in South Asia," *Journal of Strategic Studies* 38, no. 5 (May 2015): 729-72.

13 Pakistan's motives for launching the Kargil initiative are discussed in Feroz Hassan Khan, Peter R. Lavoy, and Christopher Clary, "Pakistan's Motivations and Calculations for the Kargil Conflict," in *Asymmetric Warfare*, ed. Lavoy, 64-91. Prior to the publication of Lavoy's book, many analysts argued that Pakistan's aggression was emboldened by its newly overt nuclear weapons capabilities, demonstrated in its May 1998 explosive tests. See, for example, Tellis, Fair, and Medby, *Limited Conflicts under the Nuclear Umbrella*, 48, 49 and Kapur, *Dangerous Deterrent*, 115-31. Khan, Lavoy, and Clary rebut this argument, writing that the Kargil planners "were not directly emboldened to undertake this operation because Pakistan's nuclear weapons capability was demonstrated in the previous summer. Nuclear deterrence was at best a vague notion at this point in time" (90). Also see Lavoy's "Introduction: The Importance of the Kargil Conflict," where he says, "Pakistani planners were not motivated by a calculation that the risk of nuclear escalation would deter India from counterattacking" (11). However, in a more recent analysis, Michael Cohen writes: "Much evidence suggests that Pakistani nuclear weapons were central to the Kargil plans and that the intrusion was part of a nuclear weapons-emboldened assertive foreign policy." See his *When Proliferation Causes Peace: The Psychology of Nuclear Crises* (Washington, DC: Georgetown University Press, 2017), 133. This question remains unresolved.

14 Lavoy, "Introduction," 19. John H. Gill puts the "total number of intruders," including escorts, porters, and other support personnel, at "at least 1,500–2,000." "Military Operations in the Kargil Conflict," in *Asymmetric Warfare*, ed. Lavoy, 96.

15 Gill, "Military Operations," 99.

16 In April 1984, Indian military forces occupied the Siachen Glacier in far northern Kashmir, just south of China's Xinjiang province. Pakistani forces soon followed suit, and sporadic battles have been fought between the two sides since June 1984. The glacier occupies some 1,000 square miles of territory in the Karakoram Mountains, much of which lies at elevations above 17,000 feet. The question of which country is sovereign over the Siachen Glacier is a dispute within a dispute; because both India and Pakistan claim all of Kashmir, each country also claims complete control over the glacier. The Siachen conflict has its roots in the vagueness of the 1949 Karachi Agreement, which demarcated the Cease-Fire Line between India and Pakistan after the first Kashmir war. That pact delineated the ostensibly "temporary" boundary between the Indian state of Jammu and Kashmir, and Azad ("Free") Kashmir and the Northern Areas, both held by Pakistan. When the Cease-Fire Line was drawn, roughly 40 miles of the boundary leading up to the Chinese border was left undelineated, because the area "was considered an inaccessible no-man's land." The issue remained unresolved by the Simla Agreement of 1972, which replaced the Cease-Fire Line with the new LOC without addressing the matter of the undrawn boundary. See Robert G. Wirsing, *Pakistan's Security under Zia: The Policy Imperatives of a Peripheral Asian State* (New York: St. Martin's Press, 1991), 143–94.

17 John Lancaster, "U.S. Defused Kashmir Crisis on Brink of War," *Washington Post*, July 26, 1999.

18 Ramesh Vinayak, "Nasty Surprise," *India Today International*, May 31, 1999, 21; Harinder Baweja and Ramesh Vinayak, "Peak by Peak," *India Today International*, June 14, 1999, 17-21.

19 Manoj Joshi and Harinder Baweja, "Blasting Peace," *India Today International*, June 7, 1999, 12-17. See also Gill, "Military Operations," 106-7.

20 Joshi and Baweja, "Blasting Peace"; Michael Fathers, "On the Brink," *Time*, June 7, 1999, 48-49.

21 Government of India, *From Surprise to Reckoning*, 105. For the most comprehensive evaluation of India's use of airpower during the Kargil conflict, see Benjamin S. Lambeth, *Airpower at 18,000': The Indian Air Force in the Kargil War* (Washington, DC: Carnegie Endowment for International Peace, 2012)

22 Saba Naqvi Bhaumik, "The Dove at War," *India Today International*, July 12, 1999, 26-27.

23 Lancaster, "U.S. Defused Kashmir Crisis on Brink of War."

24 Gill, "Military Operations," 105.

25 Bruce Riedel, "American Diplomacy and the 1999 Kargil Summit at Blair House," Center for the Advanced Study of India, University of Pennsylvania, Philadelphia, 2002, 4.

26 Lavoy, "Introduction," 11, note 31.

27 Tellis, Fair, and Medby, *Limited Conflicts under the Nuclear Umbrella*, 15.

28 Jaswant Singh, *A Call to Honour: In Service of Emergent India* (New Delhi: Rupa, 2006), 320.

29 Malik, *Kargil*, 259-60.

30 Gill, "Military Operations," 111. See p. 112, notes 64 and 66 for media references. For an analysis, including many instances of disorganized nuclear signaling, see Timothy D. Hoyt, "Kargil: The Nuclear Dimension," in *Asymmetric Warfare*, ed. Lavoy, 144-70. A concise overview of Kargil's nuclear dimensions is in Todd S. Sechser and Matthew Fuhrmann, *Nuclear Weapons and Coercive Diplomacy* (New York: Cambridge University Press, 2017), 147-55.

31 Manoj Joshi and Raj Chengappa, "The Marathon War," *India Today International*, June 21, 1999, 12-13.

32 Baweja and Vinayak, "Peak by Peak," 18.

33 Harinder Baweja, "Slow but Steady," *India Today International*, June 28, 1999, 21; Government of India, *From Surprise to Reckoning*, 105.

34 Malik, *Kargil*, 146-47.

35 Lavoy, "Introduction," 21. See Gill, "Military Operations," 114-19, for a detailed discussion of the Indian Army's increasingly successful efforts to dislodge the invaders.

36 Raj Chengappa, "Will the War Spread?" *India Today International*, July 5, 1999, 14-17.

37 For an overview, see Strobe Talbott, *Engaging India: Diplomacy, Democracy, and the Bomb* (Washington, DC: Brookings, 2004), 154-69.

38 Raj Chengappa, "Minefield Ahead," *India Today International*, June 7, 1999, 17.

39 Riedel, "American Diplomacy and the 1999 Kargil Summit," 4.

40 John W. Garver, "The Restoration of Sino-Indian Comity Following India's Nuclear Tests," *China Quarterly*, no. 168 (December 2001): 882.

41 Raj Chengappa, "Face-Saving Retreat," *India Today International*, July 19, 1999, 16.

42 Garver, "Sino-Indian Comity," 882.

43 Raj Chengappa, "On High Ground," *India Today International*, June 28, 1999, 25.

44 The most authoritative account of the Kargil conflict, Lavoy's *Asymmetric Warfare*, concludes that "Indian troops were within days of opening another front across the LOC and possibly the international border, an act that could have triggered a large-scale conventional military engagement, which in turn might have escalated to an exchange of recently tested Indian and Pakistani nuclear weapons." Lavoy, "Introduction," 2.

45 Chengappa, "Face-Saving Retreat," 17.

46 Riedel, "American Diplomacy and the 1999 Kargil Summit," 6.

47 Chengappa, "Will the War Spread?" 14.

48 Lancaster, "U.S. Defused Kashmir Crisis on Brink of War."

49 C. Raja Mohan, "Pak. Must Pull Out Troops," *The Hindu*, June 28, 1999.

50 Garver, "Sino-Indian Comity," 884.

51 Riedel, "American Diplomacy and the 1999 Kargil Summit," 6, 7.

52 Riedel, "American Diplomacy and the 1999 Kargil Summit," 8, 9.

53 Musharraf, *In the Line of Fire*, 97-98.

54 Riedel, "American Diplomacy and the 1999 Kargil Summit," 9-12.

55 Riedel, "American Diplomacy and the 1999 Kargil Summit," 11.

56 Raj Chengappa, *Weapons of Peace: The Secret Story of India's Quest to Be a Nuclear Power* (New Delhi: HarperCollins, 2000), 437. The three delivery systems were the Prithvi and Agni missiles, as well as the Mirage-2000 attack aircraft. Lavoy contends that "neither Pakistan nor India readied its nuclear arms for employment." "Introduction" to *Asymmetric Conflict*, 11.

57 Riedel, "American Diplomacy and the 1999 Kargil Summit," 11.

58 Riedel, "American Diplomacy and the 1999 Kargil Summit," 12.

59 "Press Briefing by Senior Administration Official on President's Meeting with Prime Minister Sharif of Pakistan," Office of the Press Secretary, The White House, July 4, 1999, http://www.fas.org/news/pakistan/1999/990704-pak-wh2.htm.

60 "India Claims Control of Key Kashmir Sector," *CNN Interactive*, July 10, 1999.

61 "India, Pakistan Agree to End Kashmir Fighting," *CNN Interactive*, July 11, 1999.

62 Nawaz Sharif, "Prime Minister's Address to the Nation," July 12, 1999, http://www.pak.gov.pk.

63 "India Says All Kashmir Infiltrators Have Retreated," *Reuters*, July 17, 1999.

64 K. Alan Kronstadt, "Pakistan–US Relations," *Issue Brief*, Congressional Research Service, Washington, DC, October 28, 2002, 9.

65 Rama Lakshmi, "India Wages a War of Words," *Washington Post*, December 19, 2001.

66 Nayak and Krepon, "U.S. Crisis Management in South Asia's Twin Peaks Crisis," 52.

67 Dennis Kux, "India's Fine Balance," *Foreign Affairs* 81, no. 3 (May–June 2002): 98-100; Sood and Sawhney, *Operation Parakram*, 73-79.

68 John Lancaster, "Pakistan to Follow India in Removing Troops from Border," *Washington Post*, October 18, 2002.

69 Kapur, *Dangerous Deterrent*, 134.

70 Hoyt, "Kargil: The Nuclear Dimension," 160, note 58.

71 John Lancaster, "India to Remove Some Forces from Border with Pakistan," *Washington Post*, October 17, 2002. The oft-quoted figure of one million Indian and Pakistani soldiers facing off against one another included troops in Kashmir.

72 Sagan and Waltz, *Spread of Nuclear Weapons*, 146. (Sagan)

73 Devin T. Hagerty, "The Nuclear Holdouts: India, Israel, and Pakistan," in *Slaying the Nuclear Dragon: Disarmament Dynamics in the Twenty-First Century*, ed. Tanya Ogilvie-White and David Santoro (Athens: University of Georgia Press, 2012), 223-24.

74 Praveen Swami, "A War to End a War: The Causes and Outcomes of the 2001–2 India-Pakistan Crisis," in *Nuclear Proliferation in South Asia: Crisis Behaviour and the Bomb*, ed. Sumit Ganguly and S. Paul Kapur (London: Routledge, 2009), 144.

75 Kanti Bajpai, "To War or Not to War: The India–Pakistan Crisis of 2001–2," in *Nuclear Proliferation in South Asia*, ed. Ganguly and Kapur, 165.

76 Rajesh Basrur, *South Asia's Cold War: Nuclear Weapons and Conflict in Comparative Perspective* (London: Routledge, 2008), 61.

77 Steve Coll, "The Stand-Off," *New Yorker*, February 13, 2006 (no p. # in online version), https:// www.newyorker.com/magazine/2006/02/13/the-stand-off, Coll adds that, "by Christmas Day of 2001, C.I.A. and other intelligence analysts in Washington had concluded that an invasion of Pakistani territory by Indian forces could escalate to nuclear conflict."

78 Nayak and Krepon, "U.S. Crisis Management in South Asia's Twin Peaks Crisis," 52, 24-25.

79 Celia W. Dugger, "Indian General Talks Bluntly of War and a Nuclear Threat," *New York Times*, January 12, 2002.

80 LeT played a small part in the Parliament attack. Tankel, *Storming the World Stage*, 112.

81 Nayak and Krepon, "U.S. Crisis Management in South Asia's Twin Peaks Crisis," 25-26.

82 Condoleezza Rice, *No Higher Honor: A Memoir of My Years in Washington* (New York: Broadway, 2011), 123.

83 MacDonald, *Defeat Is an Orphan*, 137.

84 President Pervez Musharraf's Address to the Nation, January 12, 2002, http://www.pak.gov.pk/President_Addresses/President_address.htm.

85 Edward Luce, "India Prepares for Strike on Camps," *Financial Times*, May 17, 2002.

86 Steve Coll, "Between India and Pakistan, a Changing Role for the US," *Washington Post*, May

26, 2002; Nayak and Krepon, "U.S. Crisis Management in South Asia's Twin Peaks Crisis," 19. Musharraf recalls that he "personally conveyed messages to Prime Minister Vajpayee through every international leader who came to Pakistan, that if Indian troops moved a single step across the international border or Line of Control, they should not expect a conventional war from Pakistan." Mistry, "Tempering Optimism about Nuclear Deterrence in South Asia," 171.

87   Chari, Cheema, and Cohen, *Four Crises and a Peace Process*, 154.

88   Narang, *Nuclear Strategy in the Modern Era*, 275.

89   G.V. Gireesh, "Game of Patience," *Outlook*, May 27, 2002, 34-39.

90   Rahul Roy-Chaudhury, "Nuclear Doctrine, Declaratory Policy, and Escalation Control," in *Escalation Control and the Nuclear Option in South Asia*, ed. Michael Krepon, Rodney W. Jones, and Ziad Haider (Washington, DC: Stimson Center, 2004), 109.

91   Sood and Sawhney, *Operation Parakram*, 82-83. Pakistan also moved its nuclear-capable missiles in May. Mistry, "Tempering Optimism," 172.

92   Feroz Hassan Khan, *Eating Grass: The Making of the Pakistani Bomb* (Stanford: Stanford University Press, 2012), 350.

93   Nayak and Krepon, "U.S. Crisis Management in South Asia's Twin Peaks Crisis," 55. Also see Rahul Bedi, "The Military Dynamics," *Frontline*, June 8–21, 2002.

94   Nayak and Krepon, "U.S. Crisis Management in South Asia's Twin Peaks Crisis," 33-36. A former U.S. official, Bruce Riedel, recounts that both Powell and Armitage later told him "that they thought that war was a very real danger and that if it began, it would go to the brink of nuclear war, if not over." *Avoiding Armageddon*, 151.

95   "A Surgical Strike Is the Answer," *Outlook*, June 10, 2002.

96   Nayak and Krepon, "U.S. Crisis Management in South Asia's Twin Peaks Crisis," 33.

97   Cohen, *When Proliferation Causes Peace*, 141.

98   Ganguly and Hagerty, *Fearful Symmetry*, 177-80.

99   Rahul Bedi and Anton La Guardia, "Pakistan Steps Back from Brink," *Daily Telegraph*, June 8, 2002.

100   "Musharraf: Here's What I'll Do," *Washington Post*, June 23, 2002.

101   "Spokesman Richard Boucher," State Department Daily Briefing, October 31, 2002, https://2001-2009.state.gov/r/pa/prs/dpb/2002/14832.htm

102   Lancaster, "Pakistan to Follow India in Removing Troops from Border."

103   "Musharraf: Here's What I'll Do"; "Vajpayee: Keep Your Promise," *Washington Post*, June 23, 2002; Christina B. Rocca, Assistant Secretary of State for South Asian Affairs, "Deepening US Engagement in South Asia," remarks to the American Enterprise Institute, Washington, DC, October 10, 2002.

104   Nayak and Krepon, *Unfinished Crisis*, 1; Angel Rabasa et al., *The Lessons of Mumbai* (Santa Monica, CA: RAND Corporation, 2009), 4; Riedel, *Avoiding Armageddon*, 5;

105   MacDonald, *Defeat Is an Orphan*, 203; Menon, *Choices*, 60; Tankel, *Storming the World Stage*, 215.

106 Nayak and Krepon, *Unfinished Crisis*, 6; Rabasa, *Lessons of Mumbai*, 4.

107 Rajesh Basrur et al., *The 2008 Mumbai Terrorist Attacks: Strategic Fallout* (Singapore: S. Rajaratnam School of International Studies, Nanyang Technological University, 2009), 19.

108 "Mumbai Attack Might Have Led to Ind-Pak Nuclear War: Roemer," *Indian Express*, September 1, 2011.

109 Srinath Raghavan, "Terror, Force and Diplomacy," *Economic and Political Weekly* 43, no 49 (December 6–12, 2008): 10-12; Helene Cooper, "South Asia's Deadly Dominoes," *New York Times*, December 7, 2008.

110 Rice, *No Higher Honor*, 719.

111 Saeed Shah, "Mysterious Phone Call Brought Nuclear Rivals to the Brink after Mumbai," *The Guardian*, December 7, 2008.

112 Rice, *No Higher Honor*, 720.

113 Nayak and Krepon, *Unfinished Crisis*, 12, 13.

114 Menon, *Choices*, 62.

115 Pranab Dhal Samanta, "26/11: How India Debated a War with Pakistan That November," *Indian Express*, November 26, 2010. Army Vice-Chief M.L. Naidu sat in for army chief Deepak Kapoor, who was abroad.

116 Samanta, "26/11."

117 Samanta, "26/11"; Pravin Sawhney, "Whither Our War Preparedness?" *Pioneer*, June 4, 2015.

118 Praveen Swami, "Talking to Pakistan in Its Language," *The Hindu*, June 11, 2014.

119 Swami, "Talking to Pakistan in Its Language."

120 Sawhney, "Whither Our War Preparedness?"

121 Sawhney, "Whither Our War Preparedness?"

122 Swami, "Talking to Pakistan in Its Language."

123 Samanta, "26/11."

124 Samanta, "26/11."

125 Nayak and Krepon, *Unfinished Crisis*, 44.

126 Raj Chengappa and Saurabh Shukla, "Reining in the Rogue," *India Today*, December 4, 2008; Basrur, *2008 Mumbai Terrorist Attacks*, 18; Samuel Black, "Appendix I: The Structure of South Asian Crises from Brasstacks to Mumbai," in *Crises in South Asia: Trends and Potential Consequences*, ed. Michael Krepon and Nathan Cohn (Washington, DC: Stimson Center, 2011), 52, 53.

127 Chengappa and Shukla, "Reining in the Rogue."

128 Rama Lakshmi, "Cabinet Member Resigns amid Anger in India," *Washington Post*, December 1, 2008; "Indian Defense Chief: No Plans for Military Action." *Associated Press*, December 16, 2008.

129 Chengappa and Shukla, "Reining in the Rogue." This piece quotes former Indian Army chief

V.P. Malik as saying: "Such strikes are a risky gambit," as they "can trigger a full scale war."

130 "We Feared Indian Strike: ISI Chief," *The Hindu*, January 8, 2009.

131 Riedel, *Avoiding Armageddon*, 22.

132 Basrur, *2008 Mumbai Terrorist Attacks*, 22.

133 Nayak and Krepon, *Unfinished Crisis*, 13.

134 Black, "Structure of South Asian Crises," 51.

135 Nayak and Krepon, *Unfinished Crisis*, 27.

136 Nayak and Krepon, *Unfinished Crisis*, 27-28. In the early 2000s, frustrated by their inability to punish Pakistan for its persistent subconventional aggression, Indian military planners developed ideas for conventional retaliatory options that (they hoped) would not cross Islamabad's nuclear "red lines." For more details, see George Perkovich and Toby Dalton, *Not War, Not Peace? Motivating Pakistan to Prevent Cross-Border Terrorism* (New Delhi: Oxford University Press, 2016), 73-103, and Christopher Clary and Vipin Narang, "Doctrine, Capabilities, and (In)Stability in South Asia," in *Deterrence Stability and Escalation Control in South Asia*, ed. Krepon and Thompson, 94-99. The so-called Cold Start option refers to the rapid unleashing of shallow armored incursions along a broad front, intended to seize limited territory and impose a political settlement on Pakistan. In theory, such a quick, measured response could be undertaken before third parties (e.g., the United States) can get involved in crisis management. Indian political leaders have been skeptical of these designs, and Cold Start has never been official Indian doctrine, but Pakistani military planners had repeatedly expressed to U.S. officials their concerns regarding Cold Start.

137 Nayak and Krepon, *Unfinished Crisis*, 19. Interestingly, both the external affairs minister, Mukherjee, and the foreign secretary, Shivshankar Menon, favored a military response. In addition to Nayak and Krepon, p. 19, see Menon, *Choices*, 61.

138 Nayak and Krepon, *Unfinished Crisis*, 7, 28.

139 Black, "Structure of South Asian Crises," 51.

140 Basrur, *2008 Mumbai Terrorist Attacks*, 22; Black, "Structure of South Asian Crises," 19.

141 Emily Wax and Rama Lakshmi, "As Rice Presses Pakistan, Mumbai Residents Hold Massive Rally," *Washington Post*, December 4, 2008; Black, "Structure of South Asian Crises," 51.

142 Nayak and Krepon, *Unfinished Crisis*, 42. See also Muhammad Saleh Zaafir, "India Planned Strike on Muridke after Mumbai Attacks, Reveals Kasuri," *The News International*, August 28, 2015.

143 Riedel, *Avoiding Armageddon*, 21.

144 U.S. Embassy Islamabad to Department of State, "GOI Embassy Draws Distinction between ISI and Civilian Leaders," secret cable, December 5, 2008, https://www.theguardian.com/world/2010/nov/30/pakistan-usforeignpolicy1

145 U.S. Embassy New Delhi to Department of State, "Indian Foreign Secretary: 'Huge Stake' in Special Representative Holbrooke's Success," secret cable, February 17, 2009, http://theguardian.com/world/us-embassy-cables-documents/192309

146 U.S. Embassy New Delhi to Department of State, "India Scenesetter for Special Representative Holbrooke," Secret Cable, February 12, 2009, http://theguardian.com/world/us-embassy-

cables-document/1991731

147 "Excerpts of Prime Minister Dr. Manmohan Singh's Intervention in the Lok Sabha during Discussion on the Recent Terrorist Attacks in Mumbai," New Delhi, December 11, 2008, https://www.indianembassy.org/archives_details.php?nid=940

148 Ganguly and Kapur, *India, Pakistan, and the Bomb*, 72-73.

149 Black, "Structure of South Asian Crises," 52.

150 K. Alan Kronstadt, "Terrorist Attacks in Mumbai, India, and Implications for U.S. Interests," *CRS Report for Congress*, Congressional Research Service, Washington, DC, December 19, 2008, 12.

151 Black, "Structure of South Asian Crises," 53.

152 "Pakistani Army Warns India of Response," *The Australian*, December 24, 2008.

153 Samanta, "26/11."

154 U.S. Embassy Islamabad to Department of State, "Scenesetter for Special Envoy Holbrooke," Secret Cable, February 4, 2009, http://www.theguardian.com/world/us-embassy-cables-documents/190330; Richard A. Oppel, Jr. and Salman Masood, "Pakistan Moves Troops amid Tension with India," *New York Times*, December 26, 2008.

155 Black, "Structure of South Asian Crises," 53.

156 Fayaz Bukhari and Rupam Jain, "India Mulls Response after Deadly Kashmir Attack It Blames on Pakistan," *Reuters*, September 19, 2016; Pamela Constable and Annie Gowen, "Deadly Attack in Indian Kashmir Renews 'War of Words' with Rival Pakistan," *Washington Post*, September 20, 2016; "Militants Attack an Indian Army Base," *The Economist*, September 19, 2016; George Perkovich, "India's Options in Pakistan," *Foreign Affairs*, September 21, 2016.

157 "Rising Tensions in Kashmir," *New York Times*, September 23, 2016.

158 "India Backs Off Major Retaliation," *Reuters*, September 22, 2016.

159 Praveen Swami, "Uri Terror Attack: Avoid Rash Military Action, Commanders Advise Government," *Indian Express*, September 20, 2016.

160 Shishir Gupta, "Mission LOC: How India Punished Pakistan with Surgical Strikes," *Hindustan Times*, October 3, 2016.

161 Perkovich, "India's Options in Pakistan." For another insightful examination of India's options, see Happymon Jacob, "Seven Ways to Wage War on Pakistan, Several Reasons Not to Do So," *The Wire*, September 26, 2016.

162 "Statement by His Excellency Mr. Muhammad Nawaz Sharif," General Debate of the 71st Session, UN General Assembly, September 21, 2016.

163 Shubhajit Roy, "John Kerry Spoke to Sushma Twice over Two Days," *Indian Express*, September 29, 2016.

164 Annie Gowen, "India's 'Surgical Strike' on Pakistan Territory Hints at New Era for Nuclear-Armed Rivals," *Washington Post*, September 30, 2016.

165 Pamela Constable and Shaiq Hussain, "Pakistan Prepares for a Possible Indian Attack," *Washington Post*, September 22, 2016.

166 TNN, "Pakistan Defence Minister Khawaja Muhammad Asif Threatens to Unleash Nukes Against India," *Times of India*, September 29, 2016.

167 Gupta, "Mission LOC"; Nitin A. Gokhale, "The Inside Story of India's 2016 'Surgical Strikes,'" *The Diplomat*, September 23, 2017.

168 "Transcript of Joint Briefing by MEA and MoD," Ministry of External Affairs, Government of India, New Delhi, September 29, 2016.

169 The remainder of this paragraph synthesizes the reporting of reputable journalists and media outlets, which are cited below. Precise details of the Indian assault remain scanty.

170 Gowen, "India's 'Surgical Strike'"; Gupta, "Mission LOC"; Suhasini Haidar and Kallol Bhattacherjee, "Target Terror: India Strikes across LOC," *The Hindu*, September 29, 2016; Niharika Mandhana, "India Says It Hit Terrorist Bases in Pakistan-Controlled Kashmir," *Wall Street Journal*, September 29, 2016; Manu Pubby, "Army's Daring Surgical Strike Marks Radical Change in India's Pakistan Policy," *Economic Times*, October 3, 2016; "Reversing Roles," *Economist*, October 8, 2016; Sushant Singh, "Inside the Surgical Strike," *Indian Express*, October 1, 2016.

171 See, for example, Gowen, "India's 'Surgical Strike'" and Pubby, "Army's Daring Surgical Strike."

172 "Congress Releases Dates of Cross-LOC Attacks during UPA Regime," *Hindustan Times*, October 5, 2016; Shashank Joshi, "The Line of (Out of) Control," October 4, 2016, https://shashankjoshi.wordpress.com/2016/10/04/the-line-of-out-of-control/; Siddarth Varadarajan, "Indian Surgical Strikes against Terrorists in Pakistan: What We Know, What We Don't Know," *The Wire*, September 29, 2016.

173 Manoj Joshi, "Uri Aftermath: Retaliation, With De-Escalation Built In," *The Wire*, September 29, 2016. See also: C. Raja Mohan, "Breaking Out of the Box," *Indian Express*, October 3, 2016.

174 One very experienced Indian defense correspondent argues that Modi "chose strikes across the LOC as these had been carried out before and the two armies had dealt with such situations without escalating things further." Raj Chengappa, "Game Changer," *India Today*, October 6, 2016.

175 Mandhana, "India Says It Hit Terrorist Bases." One "senior Pakistani security official" did take the opportunity to warn that if India were to initiate a war, Pakistan "could use tactical nuclear weapons." Ellen Barry and Salman Masood, "India Claims 'Surgical Strikes' across Line of Control in Kashmir," *New York Times*, September 29, 2016.

176 "Statement by NSC Spokesperson Ned Price on National Security Advisor Susan E. Rice's Call with National Security Advisor Ajit Doval of India," The White House, Washington, DC, September 28, 2016. Barry and Masood, "India Claims 'Surgical Strikes' across Line of Control in Kashmir."

177 "India Strikes Back, Carries Out Surgical Strikes on Terror Launch Pads at LOC," *Times of India*, September 29, 2016.

178 Pubby, "Army's Daring Surgical Strike."

179 ANI, "Aftermath of India's Surgical Strikes in POK," *Business Standard*, October 5, 2016.

180 "Indian and Pakistani Troops Exchange Fire in Kashmir," *Associated Press*, October 3, 2016.

181 Samanth Subramaniam, "What Actually Happened in Kashmir," *The Atlantic*, October 6, 2016.

182 Michael Krepon, "Crises in South Asia: Trends and Potential Consequences," in *Crises in South Asia*, ed. Krepon and Cohn, 8.

183 See the table in Sameer Lalwani and Hannah Haegeland, "Anatomy of a Crisis: Explaining Crisis Onset in India–Pakistan Relations," in *Investigating Crises*, ed. Lalwani and Haegeland, 35.

184 The exception, of course, was India's Kargil response, because the aggressors were on the Indian side of the LOC.

185 Devin T. Hagerty, *The Consequences of Nuclear Proliferation: Lessons from South Asia* (Cambridge, MA: MIT Press, 1998), 163.

186 Robert Jervis, "Kargil, Deterrence Theory and International Relations Theory," in *Asymmetric Warfare*, ed. Lavoy, 390.

187 There is a great deal of confusion in the literature about the nature of Pakistan's aggression at Kargil in 1999. Narang refers to Pakistan's "*conventional* aggression," arguing that "India was unable to deter Pakistan from launching a relatively aggressive *conventional* attack." *Nuclear Strategy in the Modern Era*, 253. Also see pp. 7, 11, 296. Elsewhere, Narang notes India's failure to deter "*high-level conventional* conflict, such as the Kargil War" (297) and India's inability to deter "*high-intensity* wars, such as the 1999 Kargil War" (11). Other analysts use terms like "*asymmetric* operation," Gill, "Military Operations," 123; "*limited military exercise*," Government of India, *From Surprise to Reckoning*, 236; "*limited war*," Krepon, "Crises in South Asia," 27; "*low-intensity conflict*," Rajesh M. Basrur, *Minimum Deterrence and India's Nuclear Security* (Stanford: Stanford University Press, 2006), 73-74; "*sub-conventional*" conflict, Yusuf and Kirk, "Keeping an Eye on South Asian Skies," 11-12; "*unconventional*" conflict, Tellis, Fair, and Medby, *Limited Conflicts under the Nuclear Umbrella*, xi, etc. Pakistan's covert infiltration of the Kargil area was not a conventional invasion. The territory was claimed by both countries, with the dispute between them unresolved. The NLI intruders were "lightly-equipped" paramilitary forces, "not designed for major offensive operations," who relied on "pack mules and human porters" for logistical and other needs. Gill, "Military Operations," 97-98; Khan, Lavoy, and Clary, "Pakistan's Motivations and Calculations for the Kargil Conflict," 67. They fought in local civilian garb, i.e., *shalwar kameez*. The terrain was "highly glaciated and avalanche-prone, a desolate, uninhabited desert waste of serrated, knife-edge ridges piercing the sky" at altitudes of 13–18,000 feet. This was "not a very major operation either in terms of size or capability." Government of India, *From Surprise to Reckoning*, 17, 103-4. With its forceful response, it was India that "conventionalize[d] the *unconventional* conflict." Lavoy, "Introduction," 4-5. Also see pp. 8-9, 26. Pakistan's Kargil incursion did not represent a failure of India's nuclear posture to deter a conventional invasion. (Emphases added.)

188 Samuel Black, *The Changing Political Utility of Nuclear Weapons: Nuclear Threats from 1970 to 2010* (Washington, DC: 2010), 17-18. These signals consisted of three menacing statements by Pakistani civilian and military leaders, as well as the suggestive but ambiguous nuclear-related activity discussed in the Kargil section above.

189 Devin T. Hagerty, "The Kargil War: An Optimistic Assessment," in *Nuclear Proliferation in South Asia*, ed. Ganguly and Kapur, 110. Also see: Cohen, *When Proliferation Causes Peace*, 138; Dalton and Perkovich, *India's Nuclear Options and Escalation Dominance*, 7; Gill, "Military Operations," 124; Jervis, "Kargil, Deterrence Theory and International Relations Theory," 395-96; S. Paul Kapur, "Revisionist Ambitions, Conventional Capabilities, and Nuclear Instability: Why Nuclear South Asia Is Not Like Cold War Europe," in *Inside Nuclear South Asia*, ed. Scott D. Sagan (Stanford: Stanford University Press, 2009), 197; Lambeth, *Airpower at 18,000'*, 2; Lavoy, "Introduction," 33; Sagan, in Sagan and Waltz, eds., *Spread of Nuclear Weapons*, 145-46;

Sechser and Fuhrmann, *Nuclear Weapons and Coercive Diplomacy*, 150; Waltz, in Sagan and Waltz, eds., *Spread of Nuclear Weapons*, 163.

190 Ganguly and Kapur, *India, Pakistan, and the Bomb*, 52-53

191 Sood and Sawhney, *Operation Parakram*, 70-71, 106.

192 V.P. Malik, *India's Military Conflicts and Diplomacy: An Inside View of Decision Making* (New Delhi: HarperCollins, 2013), 127.

193 Narang, *Nuclear Strategy in the Modern Era*, 271. Also see: Chari, Cheema, and Cohen, *Four Crises and a Peace Process*, 139 and Cohen, *When Proliferation Causes Peace*, 141.

194 Hagerty, "The Kargil War," 112. Musharraf's assertion that Pakistan did not have an operational nuclear weapons capability in 1999 is irrelevant in this context. At the time, Indian leaders had to assume that Pakistan *might* have such a capability.

195 Black, *Changing Political Utility of Nuclear Weapons*, 16.

196 Black, *Changing Political Utility of Nuclear Weapons*, 16-18. These signals included threatening statements by senior officials, raised alert levels, movements of ballistic missiles, ballistic missile tests, and movements of nuclear-capable aircraft.

197 Mistry, "Tempering Optimism about Nuclear Deterrence in South Asia," 174; Sood and Sawhney, *Operation Parakram*, 9.

198 Swami, "A War to End a War," 150, 145.

199 Mistry, "Tempering Optimism about Nuclear Deterrence in South Asia," 174

200 Narang, *Nuclear Strategy in the Modern Era*, 278.

201 Narang, *Nuclear Strategy in the Modern Era*, 277. Narang's analysis confirms and reinforces similar conclusions reached previously by scholars, for example: Basrur, *South Asia's Cold War*, 62; Chari, Cheema, and Cohen, *Four Crises and a Peace Process*, 160, 163, 172, 173, 182; Ganguly and Hagerty, *Fearful Symmetry*, 167-86; Kapur in Ganguly and Kapur, *India, Pakistan, and the Bomb*, 58; Dinshaw Mistry, "Complexity of Deterrence among New Nuclear States: The India–Pakistan Case," in *Complex Deterrence: Strategy in the Global Age*, ed. T.V. Paul, Patrick M. Morgan, and James J. Wirtz (Chicago, IL: University of Chicago Press, 2009), 24; Rajesh Rajagopalan, *Second Strike: Arguments about Nuclear War in South Asia* (New Delhi: Viking, 2005), 204; Sood and Sawhney, *Operation Parakram*, 83, 97, 116, 144, and Waltz, in Sagan and Waltz, eds., *Spread of Nuclear Weapons*, 171-72.

202 "Interview: Ex-Pakistani Pres. Musharraf Mulled Using Nukes Against India after 2001 Attack," *The Mainichi*, July 26, 2017.

203 Cohen, *When Proliferation Causes Peace*, 141-2.

204 Chari, Cheema, and Cohen, *Four Crises and a Peace Process*, 197.

205 Narang, *Nuclear Strategy in the Modern Era*, 279.

206 Krepon, "Crises in South Asia," 9. Singh "reportedly asked whether Pakistan could misperceive an Indian conventional strike as a nuclear one and respond by launching its own nuclear forces. No one could answer with any certainty." Perkovich and Dalton, *Not War, Not Peace?*, 2. For other endorsements of the nuclear deterrence argument, see: Rafiq Dossani and Jonah Blank, "Could the Kashmir Standoff Trigger Nuclear War," rand.org, October 7, 2016; PTI, "Pakistan's Nuclear Weapons Deterred India," *The Hindu*, March 10, 2009; and Waltz, in Sagan

and Waltz, eds., *Spread of Nuclear Weapons*, 173.

207 Black, "Structure of South Asian Crises from Brasstacks to Mumbai," 51; Black, *Changing Political Utility of Nuclear Weapons*, 15. Two of the threats involved increases in the alert levels of the Pakistan Army and PAF. One was a pointed statement by a senior Indian official.

208 Chengappa, "Game Changer."

209 Stephen P. Cohen, *Shooting for a Century: The India–Pakistan Conundrum* (Washington, DC: Brookings, 2013), 194; Ashley J. Tellis, *Are India–Pakistan Peace Talks Worth a Damn?* (Washington, DC: Carnegie Endowment for International Peace, 2017), 37, 71; Waltz in Sagan and Waltz, eds., *The Spread of Nuclear Weapons*, 172-73; Krepon, "Crises in South Asia," 11; Vipin Narang, "Posturing for Peace? Pakistan's Nuclear Postures and South Asian Stability," *International Security* 34, no. 3 (Winter 2009/2010): 64; George Perkovich, "Uri Won't Lead India to Undertake Major Military Action," rediff.com, September 21, 2016, http://carnegieendowment.org/2016/09/21/uri-won-t-lead-india-to-undertake-major-military-action-pub-64649; Toby Dalton and George Perkovich, *India's Nuclear Options and Escalation Dominance* (Washington, DC: Carnegie Endowment for International Peace, 2016), 16; Rajesh Rajagopalan, "Annex B. India's National Security Perspectives and Nuclear Weapons," in *The Strategic Chain Linking Pakistan, India, China, and the United States*, ed. Robert Einhorn and W.P.S. Sidhu (Washington, DC: Brookings, 2017), 28.

210 Secretary Kerry's meetings with Indian and Pakistani leaders at the UNGA in September 2016 were just about the least that Washington could have done. Days later, the readout of national security adviser Rice's call with her Indian counterpart was limited to condemnation of Pakistan's provocation and cross-border terrorism more generally.

211 Chari, Cheema, and Cohen, *Four Crises and a Peace Process*, 133.

212 Lavoy, "Introduction," 12; also see p. 28. Similar arguments appear in: Lavoy, "Why Kargil Did Not Produce General War," 197, 200-1; Jervis, "Kargil, Deterrence Theory and International Relations Theory," 391; Rodney Jones, "The Kargil Crisis: Lessons Learned by the United States," in *Asymmetric Warfare*, ed. Lavoy, 374: Mistry, "Tempering Optimism about Nuclear Deterrence in South Asia," 156; and Yusuf and Kirk, "Keeping an Eye on South Asian Skies, 7, 11.

213 Krepon, "Crises in South Asia," 13. See pp. 20-26 for an overview of U.S. crisis-management efforts during all of the cases through Mumbai. Several detailed accounts of Twin Peaks and the Mumbai episode document the important role of U.S. diplomacy in helping to dampen India's understandable desire to punish Pakistan. On Twin Peaks, see Bajpai, "To War or Not to War," 163, 171, 175-77; Chari, Cheema, and Cohen, *Four Crises and a Peace Process*, 149; Mistry, "Tempering Optimism about Nuclear Deterrence in South Asia," 163-75; Narang, *Nuclear Strategy in the Modern Era*, 275; Nayak and Krepon, "U.S. Crisis Management in South Asia's Twin Peaks Crisis," 37-43. On Mumbai, see Nayak and Krepon, *Unfinished Crisis*, 53.

214 Mistry, "Tempering Optimism about Nuclear Deterrence in South Asia," 149. See also pp. 162 and 168.

215 Mistry, "Tempering Optimism about Nuclear Deterrence in South Asia," 149, 153, 160, 171, 174, 175, 176, 177. Another problem is Mistry's contention that we need to "focus on the principal events responsible for de-escalation at the time de-escalation occurs rather than on the extended period of the entire crisis," which is methodologically dubious. The impact of nuclear weapons or the conventional military balance is logically pertinent throughout the crisis, not at one particular threshold moment. If, for example, Pakistan's nuclear posture takes

a large Indian conventional thrust off the table at the outset, that impacts all of the Indian decisions during the rest of the crisis. The shadow of nuclear weapons is a constant over time; it does not go on and off.

216 Mistry, "Tempering Optimism about Nuclear Deterrence in South Asia," 172.

217 Mistry, "Complexity of Deterrence," 186.

218 Tellis, *Are India–Pakistan Peace Talks Worth a Damn?*, 36.

219 Ladwig, "Indian Military Modernization and Conventional Deterrence in South Asia," 21-31; Clary, "Deterrence Stability and the Conventional Balance of Forces in South Asia," 141-52.

220 Narang, *Nuclear Strategy in the Modern Era*, 281. Tellingly, Ladwig's 2015 analysis of conventional deterrence in South Asia examines only limited Indian attack options, given the implausibility of larger operations in the shadow of nuclear weapons. "Indian Military Modernization," 8-9.

221 Ali Ahmed writes: "Since the mid-1990s, a large proportion of the army has been deployed in Kashmir, perhaps over a third. Even though the army in the period acquired a third strike corps, Pakistan succeeded in bogging down in Kashmir any surplus conventional advantage India might have gained, thereby neutralising India's conventional edge." "Corrosive Impact of Army's Commitment in Kashmir," *Economic and Political Weekly*, February 25, 2017.

222 Ladwig, "Indian Military Modernization," 16-17.

223 Ladwig notes that while force ratios vary, "in any instance the margin of India's local force advantage is not decisive." He puts the Indian manpower advantage in the Western theater at 1.1-1.2:1, well short of the 2:1 or higher ratios that would be preferable. He also puts the Indian advantage in tanks at 1.1:1 and "modern, high-performance main battle tanks" at 1.3:1, again much lower than Indian military planners would prefer. Ladwig, "Indian Military Modernization," 27-30. Clary estimates that the ratio of combat power "may be closer to 1:1 at the theater level on day 1 of conflict than it is to 2:1. "Deterrence Stability," 159-60, note 84.

224 Shashank Joshi, "The Mythology of Cold Start," *New York Times*, November 4, 2011; MacDonald, *Defeat Is an Orphan*, 135-37; Ladwig, "Indian Military Modernization," 6; "Guns and Ghee," *The Economist*, September 24, 2016.

225 Sood and Sawhney, *Operation Parakram*, 158-59, 77, 170, 145.

226 Government of India, *From Surprise to Reckoning*, 77.

227 MacDonald, *Defeat Is an Orphan*, 136.

228 Perkovich and Dalton, *Not War, Not Peace?*, 8.

229 Siddarth Srivastava, "Indian Army 'Backed Out' of Pakistan Attack," *Asia Times Online*, January 21, 2009.

230 Ladwig, "Indian Military Modernization," 7.

231 Samanta, "26/11."

232 Ladwig, "Indian Military Modernization," 6.

233 Sawhney, "Whither Our War Preparedness?" On India's "effective conventional parity" with Pakistan, see Manoj Joshi, "Why Things Will Likely be All Quiet on the Western Front," *The Wire*, September 26, 2016.

234 Dasgupta and Cohen, "Is India Ending Its Strategic Restraint Doctrine?" 163-77; Cohen and Dasgupta, *Arming without Aiming*, especially ix-xiii and 1-28; Shidore, "India's Strategic Culture and Deterrence Stability on the Subcontinent"; Ali Ahmed, *India's Doctrine Puzzle: Limiting War in South Asia* (New Delhi: Routledge, 2014), 110, 115-50.

235 Cohen and Dasgupta, *Arming without Aiming*, xiii, 1.

236 Dasgupta and Cohen, "Is India Ending Its Strategic Restraint Doctrine?," 163.

237 Cohen and Dasgupta, *Arming without Aiming*, 147.

238 Shidore, "India's Strategic Culture," 119, 135.

239 Shidore, "India's Strategic Culture," 135.

240 Presentation at the Carnegie Endowment for International Peace, Washington, DC, January 23, 2015.

241 Shidore, "India's Strategic Culture," 133-35. With respect to Twin Peaks, Shidore also cites nuclear deterrence and U.S. crisis management as other causes of Indian restraint. On Mumbai, he argues that "there is no evidence that the Cabinet Committee on Security seriously considered a military response" (134). This is refuted by first-person accounts, including Menon, *Choices*, 60-81.

242 Alastair Iain Johnston, *Cultural Realism: Strategic Culture and Grand Strategy in Chinese History* (Princeton, NJ: Princeton University Press, 1995). Johnston differentiates between a country's "symbolic set" and its "operational set." The former is a "symbolic or idealized set of assumptions and ranked preferences"; the latter "reflects [a] hardpolitik strategic culture [arguing] that the best way of dealing with security threats is to eliminate them through the use of force." x.

243 Ahmed, *India's Doctrine Puzzle*, 130, 150. For a particularly convincing critique of the "strategic restraint" logic in South Asia's pre-nuclear era, see Rudra Chaudhuri, "Indian 'Strategic Restraint' Revisited: The Case of the 1965 India–Pakistan War," *India Review* 17, no. 1 (March 2018): 55-75.

244 Gill, "Military Operations," 114-19, especially 115; Rajesh Rajagopalan, "India: The Logic of Assured Retaliation," in *The Long Shadow: Nuclear Weapons and Security in 21st Century Asia*, ed. Muthiah Alagappa (Stanford: Stanford University Press, 2008), 204.

245 For a more complete summary of Indian military activities, see Ahmed, *India's Doctrine Puzzle*, 129.

246 Dasgupta and Cohen, "Is India Ending Its Strategic Restraint Doctrine?" 166-67.

247 Chari, Cheema, and Cohen, *Four Crises and a Peace Process*, 139.

248 MacDonald, *Defeat Is an Orphan*, 144.

249 Vipin Narang, "The Lines That Have Been Crossed," *The Hindu*, October 4, 2016.

250 Ankit Panda and Vipin Narang, "Nuclear Stability, Conventional Instability: North Korea and the Lessons from Pakistan," November 20, 2017, https://warontherocks.com/2017/11/nuclear-stability-conventional-instability-north-korea-lessons-pakistan/.

251 Devin T. Hagerty, "India's Evolving Nuclear Posture," *Nonproliferation Review* 21, no. 3–4 (September–December 2014): 307-8.

Foreign Assistance in India's Foreign Policy: Political and Economic Determinants

Eswaran Sridharan

*University of Pennsylvania Institute for
the Advanced Study of India, New Delhi*
esridharan@yahoo.co.in

Aashik Jain

MetLife GOSC
uraashik@gmail.com

ABSTRACT

This paper describes and analyzes the emerging Indian development cooperation program in the context of India's foreign relations and policy. The paper begins by situating India and other emerging donors in the international aid architecture. It then analyzes the Indian program in terms of the key questions—how much, to whom, for what, how, and why?—focusing on the quantum, direction, modalities, institutions, and, crucially, motivations. It describes in detail the relationships with the main recipients in South Asia, Afghanistan, Myanmar, and with Africa, situating the assistance program in the larger political and security context of India's foreign policy and India's trade and investment relationships. It is argued that the Indian development cooperation program's South Asian regional and extended neighborhood focus is largely politically and security-motivated and the emerging shift in focus to Africa is for long-term relationship building rather than immediately correlated with trade and investment relationships. The program does not impose macroeconomic policy conditions but is largely tied to Indian-sourced supplies.

Keywords: South Asia, Sub-Saharan Africa, policy, security, foreign aid, partnership

RESUMEN

Este documento describe y analiza el emergente programa de cooperación para el desarrollo de la India en el contexto de las relaciones y la política exteriores. El documento empieza al situar a India y otros donantes emergentes en la arquitectura de la ayuda internacional. Luego analiza el programa indio en términos de las preguntas clave: ¿cuánto, a quién, para qué, cómo y por qué? - centrándose en la cantidad, la dirección, las modalidades, las instituciones y, fundamentalmente, las motivaciones. Describe detalladamente las relaciones con los principales destinatarios en Asia del Sur, Afganistán, Myanmar y África, situando el programa de asistencia en el contexto político y de seguridad más amplio de la política exterior de la India y las relaciones comerciales y de inversión de la India. Se argumenta que el enfoque regional y extendido de Asia del Sur del programa de cooperación para el desarrollo es en gran medida motivado por la política y la seguridad y el cambio emergente en África es para la construcción de relaciones a largo plazo en lugar de correlacionarse inmediatamente con las relaciones comerciales y de inversión. El programa no impone condiciones macroeconómicas, pero está primordialmente ligado a los suministros obtenidos por India.

Palabras clave: Asia meridional, África subsahariana, política, seguridad, ayuda exterior, asociación

摘要

本文在印度外交关系和政策的背景下描述并分析了印度新兴发展合作计划。本文首先将印度和其他国际援助框架下的新兴援助者进行了联系。之后针对印度计划的几个关键问题进行了分析——计划规模是多少？针对谁？目的是什么？如何做？为什么做？——这几个问题聚焦于量度、方向、方式、制度、以及动机（尤为关键）。本文详细描述了印度援助的主要接受者——它们来自南亚、阿富汗、缅甸、以及非洲，同时将援助计划置于印度外交政策和贸易投资关系的政治背景和安全背景之中（进行考量）。本文主张，印度发展合作计划中有关南亚区域和"大周边"（extended neighbour-hood）这一焦点在很大程度上受到了政治和安全因素的影响，并且该计划最近将焦点转变到非洲的目的是为了建立长期关系，而不是立即建立贸易投资关系。此计划并没有推行宏观经济政策形势，但它却在很大程度上和印度政策有关。

关键词：南亚，亚撒哈拉非洲，政策，安全，外交援助，伙伴关系

Introduction: Key Questions about India as an Emerging Donor

Emerging economies are also emerging as aid donors and players in the international aid architecture and in the use of aid as a foreign policy tool. India's development partnership policy has been little studied for a country that is a major emerging market and regional power and has given over $34 billion (bn) in aid since 2004. This paper attempts a detailed account and analysis of India as an emerging foreign aid donor, or development partner as it prefers to call itself while rejecting the former term (I will refer to Indian assistance rather than aid henceforth). It analyzes India's development partnership program within the framework of Indian foreign policy and relations rather than that of only the development aid literature. India is not a member of the Development Assistance Committee (DAC) of the Organization for Economic Cooperation and Development (OECD), the traditional coordination mechanism of the developed country donors and the international aid regime. This paper will analyze India's development partnership policy in the context of its foreign policy by asking and analyzing five key questions:

1. *How much?* Aid numbers have always been prone to massaging as donors attempt to show their largesse. A good handle on India's assistance numbers is an essential first step.

2. *To Whom?* What have been the allocations by country and/or region? To what extent is Indian assistance directed to the "near abroad" versus more geographically distant countries? Is the assistance directed to the poorest countries or to resource-rich countries?

3. *For what?* What are the purposes to which this assistance is directed? What are the sectors and types of projects being assisted? Is there a discernible philosophy regarding economic development in Indian assistance policy?

4. *How?* What are the modalities and institutional mechanisms through which Indian assistance works? Is it through grants or loans? Is it tied to imports from the donor? Which arms of the government give the assistance and how is it coordinated and administered? Is India's assistance strategically planned, either for promoting development or for promoting its interests, or it is *ad hoc*, case by case, and evolving?

5. *Why?* What are the motivations of this assistance? Is it to secure access to scarce natural resources, commercial expansion, or for geo-strategic goals or in response to geo-political competitive dynamics? Is it coordinated with India's expanding trade and investment relationships? This paper links India's program to its foreign policy toward all its major recipients with a section on each.

Emerging Donors in the International Aid Architecture

While the post-war global foreign aid regime has been largely constructed and driven by Western countries, other country groups also played a varying role. For a few decades, the Soviet Union (and Maoist China despite low per capita income) was an important player in countries allied to its interests. After the first oil-shock of 1973, some of the OPEC did so in the 1970s (especially Kuwait, Saudi Arabia, and Venezuela), through both bilateral and multilateral institutions (such as the OPEC Fund for International Development) targeted especially to members of the Organization of the Islamic Conference (OIC) and global-membership multilateral institutions (notably IFAD and UNIDO). But, with the sharp decline in oil prices in the 1980s, the economic power of OPEC diminished and with it reduced any influence they might have on the global aid regime.

However, today the economic resurgence of non-Western countries, epitomized by the emergence of China and of the other BRICS (the Brazil–Russia–India–China–South Africa group), the BRICS-promoted New Development Bank (NDB), and the Chinese-promoted Asian Infrastructure Investment Bank (AIIB), is raising new questions, challenges, and perhaps even hope about the future of the global aid regime. India, like China earlier, graduated from International Development Association (IDA)—the largest multilateral concessional source of development aid—in 2014, and after a period of transitional support till 2017, is now off it completely, borrowing at standard World Bank interest rates. It is an emerging donor.

Currently, the international aid architecture is, to simplify a bit, constituted by two broad groups of donors (for useful outlines of the international aid regime and emerging donors, see Manning 2006; Naim 2007; Paulo and Reisen 2010; Six 2009; Walz and Ramachandran 2011; Woods 2008).

First, the traditional developed-country donors who coordinate their aid policies through the OECD's DAC, formed in 1960. The DAC defines Official Development Assistance (ODA or aid) as a concessional transaction (a minimum of 25 percent must be a grant, calculated for loans at a 10 percent reference rate), that is concessional loans and grants provided by governments for the promotion of economic development and welfare and including technical cooperation (Chaturvedi 2008, 5). DAC ODA enjoyed near-total dominance in the 1990s, but the pattern has changed since the 2000s. ODA from DAC donors in 2016 was $145 bn (Table 1). DAC ODA as a percentage of GNI declined from 0.51 percent (1960) to 0.22 percent (2000) before recovering to 0.32 percent (2016) (Table 1).

Second, a diverse non-DAC group of emerging donors, which include China, India, Brazil, South Africa, Russia, and Venezuela among others, have emerged in the 2000s. Manning (2006) has identified four subgroups of the non-DAC donors: (i) OECD mem-

Table 1. DAC ODA (Official Development Assistance) 1960–2017

Year	ODA (U.S.D. Mn)	ODA as a Percent of GNI
1960	4,676	0.51
1970	6,713	0.33
1980	26,304	0.35
1990	52,808	0.33
2000	54,021	0.22
2010	128,484	0.32
2012	127,030	0.29
2013	134,847	0.30
2014	137,139	0.29
2015	131,563	0.30
2016	144,965	0.32
2017(p)	146,600	NA

Source: OECD, accessed July 11, 2018—http://www.oecd.org/dac/stats/data.htm

Note:

1. (p) is for preliminary; NA is for not available

2. The values are basis current prices (last updated April 9, 2018)

3. For raw data, see the file "Longterm-ODA" and "TAB01e"

bers not part of DAC; (ii) EU members from Central and Eastern Europe that are not part of the OECD; (iii) Middle East and other OPEC; (iv) "others" that do not fall into the above three categories (including China and India).

Of the third subgroup above, mainly the oil-rich Arab donors, while these are not members of the OECD's DAC most report their aid to the DAC although not necessarily according to DAC definitions or disaggregation (for example, do not report debt forgiveness as ODA unlike DAC). Arab aid started in the 1970s, with five aid agencies being established between 1971 and 1976, led by the United Arab Emirates (UAE), Saudi Arabia, and Kuwait. The average net aid for these three states between 1973 and 2008 was 1.5 percent of GNI, and between 1973 and 1994, Arab aid accounted for 13.5 percent of global ODA (Walz and Ramachandran 2011). Arab aid tends to flow to other Arab and Muslim countries, but in recent years to sub-Saharan Africa too.

The fourth subgroup of non-DAC donors referred to above tends to call their aid development assistance or cooperation, and to focus on infrastructure, particularly China, and particularly to Africa. The main southern donors tend to be regional powers—China, India, Brazil, and South Africa. Although aid from this group does not impose policy conditions, the majority of their aid is tied to the use of donor-country goods and services, contractors or oil imports or packaged with commercial deals and foreign direct investment in an era when DAC aid is moving to untied aid. Aid from this group of countries is much less transparent as regards data and disaggregation. Non-DAC donor ODA in 2015 (excluding India and China) was $17.55 bn, of which $12 bn was from Saudi Arabia and UAE compared to DAC aid of $131 bn that year.[1]

The evolution of the international aid regime in the past quarter century can be summarized as follows. Following a decline in the 1980s, the era of Third World debt, aid flows began rising again in the 1990s. The traditional donors pledged to reform the aid architecture, creating the Paris Declaration on Aid Effectiveness in the Paris High-level Forum, 2005, followed by the Accra Agenda for Action in 2008. This was supposed to usher in a revised architecture that prioritized commitments to improve (recipient) ownership, alignment, harmonization, results, and mutual accountability. This is now the basis of the OECD-DAC approach to ODA. However, the Paris Forum was attended by many new donors (notably, not India, but India signed on in 2006). However, there has been not much progress in implementing all the commitments made in the Paris Declaration and Accra Agenda, even by DAC donors. Since the Fourth High-level Forum on Aid Effectiveness of November 2011 in Busan, South Korea, DAC donors have been trying to extend their lending norms to new donors but with diverse results to date.

These developments have led to the construction of the so-called Southern model (De Renzio and Seifert 2014) which does not impose DAC economic criteria, philosophies, and conditionalities. However, on a closer look, the Southern model collapses into a diversity of donors and practices. Comparatively speaking, Chinese assistance is much larger than India's and its motivations have shifted from ideological to mutual economic interests, resource access, and energy security (Gu et al. 2016). Non-DAC aid on the whole tends to be geopolitically motivated somewhat like Western aid was at an early stage during the Cold War; perhaps it will evolve as it matures as Western aid did toward the current OECD-DAC approach referred to in the last paragraph, less nakedly geopolitical and more embedded in development economics, but that remains to be seen.

India: Emerging Development Partnership Policies

Historical Background and Evolution

Historically, India's assistance to fellow developing countries began in 1949 with scholarships and humanitarian assistance in cases of famine.[2] The Colombo Plan was the main channel for scholarships, although India's own International Technical and Economic Cooperation (ITEC) program started in 1964 for training and transfer of expertise. Nepal and Bhutan were the earliest recipients of Indian assistance and from 1959, India has been giving program-based assistance as annual grants to these countries, worked into their and India's five-year plans.

Indian assistance has traditionally been coordinated by two ministries, the Ministry of External Affairs (MEA) and the Ministry of Finance's Department of Economic Affairs (DEA) (see Agrawal 2007; Chanana 2009; Chaturvedi 2012a, 2012b, 2008; Kragelund 2010; Mullen 2012, 2013; Naidu 2008; Price 2005, for accounts of India's emerging assistance policies). The MEA concentrates on neighbors like Nepal, Bhutan, and other South Asian countries, for immediate geopolitical reasons of keeping them from aligning against India, and gave mainly grants and lines of credit (LOC) (through the Exim Bank since 2004–05), and also assistance through the ITEC program.

ITEC, which came into existence in 1964, operates through four modalities: training in India, project assistance, study trips, and humanitarian assistance. The DEA (in the Ministry of Finance) gave LOC to a range of developing countries, especially South Asian neighbors.

Exim Bank LOC

There was a basic policy shift from 2003 to 2004 from government to government credit lines to government-supported LOC through the Exim Bank of India. As the Ministry of Finance put it:

> Policy on Lines of Credit: For about four decades, Department of Economic Affairs on behalf of Government of India had been extending lines of credit (LOCs) to friendly developing foreign countries. These LOCs were essentially "Government to Government" (G to G) credit lines as the credit agreements were signed between GOI and the Government of the recipient country. Till 2003–04, the LOCs were from Government to Government. Accordingly the full amount covered by the LOCs, used to be provided in the Budget. Since 2003–04, this system has been substituted by extending GOI supported Lines of Credit through Exim Bank of India.[3]

To address a question that can be raised, at the outset, viz., why should LOC be considered foreign assistance and not commercial activity? The answer is that it is government-subsidized and below market rates of interest:

Furthermore, the Ministry of Finance continues:

Q. What is the interest rate the overseas importer of Indian goods has to pay?

A. The overseas importer of Indian goods has to approach the overseas borrower financial institution/recipient of Exim Bank's LOC, for approval of his proposal for import of Indian goods on deferred credit terms. The interest rate that the importer will need to pay to the recipient of Exim Bank's LOC, will depend on various factors such as the cost of fund, the currency of credit, tenure of credit, security offered by the importer, the risk perception of the importer and the interest rate structure prevalent in the country. It may however be mentioned that Exim Bank's interest rates on LOCs being competitive, the importer would normally have to pay interest rate lower than what he would otherwise pay to his Bank on similar credits.[4]

The last sentence indicates that the LOCs of the Exim Bank may be considered subsidized credit and hence foreign assistance. The interest subsidy on the Exim Bank's LOCs is given in the IDEAS line item in Statement 11 of the annual Expenditure Budget.

A key turning point in Indian foreign assistance was the decision in 2003 to repay its bilateral debt to all but four countries, not to accept tied aid in the future and accept bilateral aid from only five countries and the EU, and simultaneously shift from a major aid recipient to donor (Chaturvedi 2008, 26–29). Between 2003 and 2004 and June 2018, India provided $22,515 million (m) in 227 operative Exim Bank LOCs with another $1,782 m in the pipeline to be operationalized, totaling 246 LOCs of $24,297 m (Table 2). The average worth of an operative LOC was $99 m.

Region-wise and country-wise (Table 3), 158 LOCs (of 227 operational) worth $9,229 m went to sub-Saharan Africa (henceforth, Africa refers to sub-Saharan, that is, non-Arab Africa, plus Sudan and Djibouti, and including the island states of Madagascar, Mauritius, and Seychelles), 15 LOCs worth $10,481 m to South Asian countries, 10 LOCs worth $539 m to Myanmar, 15 LOCs worth $538 m to Southeast Asia and Pacific (other than Myanmar), LOCs worth $1,167 m to the (non-oil) Middle East and Central Asia, and 22 LOCs worth 405 m to Latin America and the Caribbean. Thus, 70 percent of the number of LOCs went to Africa and 7 percent to South Asia, 4 percent to Myanmar, and 7 percent to Southeast Asia and Pacific. By value, 47 percent went to South Asia and 41 percent to Africa, these two regions getting 88 percent of the total amount loaned.

Table 2. Operating Exim Bank LOC as on June 2018

Level of Utilization of LOC	No. of LOCs	Amount ($ Mn)
Operating	227	22,515
Pipeline	19	1,782
Total	246	24,297
Of the operating		
Fully used*	142	5,762
Partly used**	43	4,793
Totally unused***	42	11,960

* Assuming amount left for utilization is zero, where such data is missing in relevant columns
** Of partly used, the amount left for utilization is $2,357.46 m
*** "To be made effective" are clubbed under this

Source: EXIM Bank, accessed July 11, 2018—http://www.eximbankindia.in/lines-of-credit

Table 3. Region-wise (Operating) LOC as on June 2018

Country/Region	No. of LOCs	Amount ($ Mn)
Africa	158	9,229
Eurasia	2	156
LAC	22	405
Middle East and Central Asia	5	1,167
Myanmar	10	539
South Asia	15	10,481
South East Asia and Pacific	15	538
TOTAL	227	22,515

Source: EXIM Bank of India, accessed July 11, 2018—http://www.eximbankindia.in/lines-of-credit

By major purpose (Table 4), the largest single number of LOCs was 71 (of 227 operational LOCs, 31 percent of the total number), covering a wide range of miscellaneous purposes too diverse to slot into sectors, worth $3,409 m, or 15 percent of the total amount of credit extended. By identifiable purpose, the loans show a focus on power and electrification, railways, agriculture, and sugar, or more generally, electricity, transport, and agriculture. The largest amounts loaned by major sector were in power projects ($1,688 m in 27 LOCs) and the related area of rural electrification ($1,646 m in 26 LOCs), the latter two between them $3,334 m or 15 percent of the total amount equaling the Miscellaneous category. There was also a significant category of general purpose LOCs which the recipient could use for any purpose, amounting to $11,070 in 40 LOCs, or 18% of the LOCs, totaling 49% of the total loaned amount.

Table 4. Purpose-wise (Operating) LOC as on June 2018

Purpose	No. of LOCs	Amount ($ Mn)	Amount Left for Utilization ($ Mn)
General	40	11,070	10,580
Agricultural	29	1,162	455
Cement	6	157	46
Rural electrification	26	1,646	921
Power	27	1,688	653
Sugar industry	11	905	29
Railway	14	1,979	816
Non-bilateral	3	500	155
Miscellaneous	71	3,409	666
Total	227	22,515	14,321

Source: EXIM Bank, accessed July 11, 2018—http://www.eximbankindia.in/lines-of-credit

Grants and Loans Other Than Through the Exim Bank

Other than the LOCs extended by the Exim Bank and subsidized by the government since 2004–05, India provided a grand total of $15,030 m in grants and loans over the period from 1984 to 2018 (Tables 5A and 5B), of which $13,364 m was over 1997–2018, particularly since 2004–05 and more so over 2008–18. Grants have dominated this non-Exim Bank assistance (77 percent) over the period 1997–2018 (Table 5A). Table 6 gives the amount of grant and loan assistance, other than Exim Bank, to South Asia. For the period since 2004–05, this totaled $7,796.

Table 5A. India's Bilateral Aid, Excluding EXIM Bank LOCs, 1997–2018 (U.S.D. Mn)

Year	Plan			Non-Plan			Total
	Grant	Loan	Total	Grant	Loan	Total	
1997–98	10	6	16	91	43	134	150
1998–99	44	27	71	100	30	131	202
1999–00	57	36	92	88	33	121	213
2000–01	76	44	120	88	38	127	247
2001–02	50	34	84	110	34	144	228
2002–03	69	44	114	56	113	169	282
2003–04	99	66	165	155	60	215	381
2004–05	101	62	164	208	65	273	437
2005–06	100	63	162	287	39	326	488
2006–07	41	8	49	305	28	333	382
2007–08	63	12	75	359	17	376	451
2008–09	73	25	98	313	177	490	588
2009–10	89	63	151	328	26	353	505
2010–11	69	106	175	495	—	495	670
2011–12	64	165	229	451	52	503	732
2012–13	86	209	296	601	129	729	1,025
2013–14	209	241	450	659	26	684	1,134
2014–15	231	380	611	678	—	678	1,289
2015–16	314	511	825	776	25	801	1,626
2016–17	—	—	—	810	—	810	810
2017–18	—	—	—	696	—	696	696
2018–19*	—	—	—	828	—	828	828
Total	1,845	2,102	3,947	8,482	935	9,416	13,364

Note: Rupee figures converted at average annual rupee–dollar exchange rates

Source: *Ministry of External Affairs, accessed July 11, 2018*—http://indiabudget.nic.in/previousub.asp

*Budget estimates

Table 5B. India's Bilateral Aid, Excluding EXIM Bank LOCs, 1984–1997 (U.S.D. Mn)

Year	Grant	Loan	Total
1984–85	85	58	143
1985–86	81	59	140
1986–87	67	206	273

1987–88	129	36	165
1988–89	124	34	158
1989–90	96	10	106
1990–91	123	49	173
1991–92	67	15	82
1992–93	50	16	66
1993–94	53	22	75
1994–95	48	25	73
1995–96	78	31	110
1996–97	73	30	102
Total	**1,074**	**593**	**1,666**

Source: Government of India, Ministry of Finance: Expenditure Budget, 1984–1997 accessed November 20, 2015

Note: Rupee figures converted at average annual rupee–dollar exchange rates

Table 6. Loans and Grants to South Asia, 1984–2019

Year	South Asia Total ($Mn U.S.D.)
1984–85	107
1985–86	105
1986–87	110
1987–88	77
1988–89	82
1989–90	54
1990–91	77
1991–92	39
1992–93	47
1993–94	45
1994–95	34
1995–96	63
1996–97	59
1997–98	89
1998–99	79
1999–00	78
2000–01	84
2001–02	95

2002–03	92
2003–04	102
2004–05	116
2005–06	145
2006–07	188
2007–08	199
2008–09	328
2009–10	349
2010–11	463
2011–12	562
2012–13	788
2013–14	902
2014–15	929
2015–16	1,184
2016–17	602
2017–18	481
2018–19*	560

Source: Government of India, Ministry of Finance: Expenditure Budget, accessed July 12, 2018—http://indiabudget.nic.in/previousub.asp

South Asia includes Nepal, Bangladesh, Bhutan, Maldives, and Sri Lanka.

*Budget estimates

Of the grand total, since 1997, or $13,364 m, $7,796, or 58 percent (Tables 5A and 6), went to its South Asian neighbors. Thus, India's non-Exim Bank Non-Plan grants and loans have gone mainly as grants, and primarily to its South Asian neighbors, with Afghanistan registering a presence since 2008–09 and Africa since 2005–06. Infrastructure, health, and education are the main focus of Indian development assistance in South Asia while assistance tied to purchases of Indian goods and services and technical training of civil servants and public sector managers is the main focus in Africa. An Indian company, usually a public sector company, has to be the lead contractor and 75 percent of goods and services should be sourced from India. However, there is an open bidding process among Indian companies and the choice of contractor among them is the host government prerogative.

Consolidated data on the number of scholarships and training slots offered under the ITEC program and allied programs like the Technical Co-operation Scheme (TCS) of the Colombo Plan, and the Special Commonwealth Assistance to Africa Program (SCAAP), and the amounts spent on these, are still unavailable. However, in

2017–18, 10,918 civilian and 2,512 defense training slots were available for 161 partner countries including 4,700 for African countries.[5]

Overall, it is not surprising, as we shall see later, that South Asia, as well as the "near abroad," including Myanmar and Afghanistan, has dominated Indian foreign assistance. However, Africa has emerged as a major focus particularly since 2008 (Duclos 2012; Kragelund 2010; Naidu 2008).

Recent Institutional and Policy Evolution: The Development Partnership Administration

In terms of institutions, organization, and strategy, in common with many other donor countries, there was considerable bureaucratic competition between the Finance Ministry and the MEA on institutional control. A proposal for an integrated agency called the India International Development and Cooperation Agency, mulled over since 2003 and mooted in the budget for 2007–08, did not come into being immediately. However, since January 2012, a Development Partnership Administration (DPA) has been formed within the MEA, and started functioning from June 2012 in effect, coordinating the implementation of India's development partnership program. It is a three-division department. The DPA currently has a staff strength of 75–80. This was a somewhat belated response to India's development assistance program since 2003–04 outpacing the support infrastructure in the

MEA. The creation of the DPA within the MEA to coordinate Indian assistance has to be seen in the context of the clear understanding in the MEA that a capital-hungry country like India can justify a foreign assistance program only if it serves vital national interests, political, strategic, and economic.[6] Foreign assistance is clearly seen as a matter of foreign policy rather than disinterested development assistance despite it not laying down economic policy conditionalities.

The core DPA mandate consists of (a) focused attention on projects, the flagship project of the DPA being the construction of 50,000 houses for displaced persons in the North and East of Sri Lanka; (b) developing a skill base; (c) helping in policy formulation. However, it is an implementation agency, not a policy-making agency and does not propagate any particular development philosophy or strategy. Policy is handled by the country desk in the relevant political (territorial) division in the MEA. The traditional mechanism continues, that is, requests for assistance originate from the would-be recipient country. The Indian embassy, usually the ambassador or deputy chief of mission, is approached by the foreign government. This also happens very commonly on high-level visits to India either by heads of government or foreign ministers, or other cabinet ministers such as trade ministers, or when Indian leaders undertake high-level visits.

Four major examples are the India–Africa Forum summits of 2008,

2011, and 2015, the Afghan president's visit to India in 2011, and the Indian prime minister's visit to Bangladesh in 2017, all of which were followed by major increases in assistance commitments. The requests are processed by the country desk, i.e., the political (territorial) division of the MEA, which makes a decision on whether and how to respond. Assistance requests and hence, assistance decisions reflected in annual numbers are not—and cannot realistically be expected to be—a smooth affair but jerky and politically punctuated. Except for long-term Plan assistance to countries like Bhutan and Nepal, one can expect the numbers to jump up and down with events.

Once a policy decision is made by the relevant political division of the MEA, the DPA is then charged with implementing the decision. After the shift to Exim Bank LOCs for project loans, including import of Indian equipment, the MEA now gives 95 percent of the total assistance, reflected in Statement 11 of the Government of India's Expenditure Budget, with about 5 percent coming from some other ministries such as Science and Technology, Health, and Renewable Energy. The factors that will shape the likely mix of bilateral and multilateral modes of Indian development partnership are unclear and need better understanding, particularly with India's future participation in new institutions like the (BRICS') NDB and the AIIB.

The experience of various DAC donor agencies and their relationship to their respective foreign ministries is being studied, particularly the models of the Japan International Cooperation Agency (JICA), UK's Department for International Development (DFID), and the US Agency for International Development (USAID). The DPA has observed that the independently spun-off DFID in the UK developed tensions with the Foreign and Commonwealth Office, and that USAID is gradually being reintegrated into the State Department.

Internal issues that the DPA is currently addressing include: (a) budget allocations—funds are needed early in the financial year; (b) the approval process—an empowered committee is proposed to be set up to speed up LOCs selected by host countries; (c) efforts to move away from the monopolization of projects by a few companies and reduce over-dependence on public enterprises; (d) streamlining contracting/procurement procedures.

India is striving to emerge as a South–South cooperation leader, co-founding the Global Network of Exim Banks and Development Finance Institutions in 2006, promoting the establishment of the Development Cooperation Forum in 2007, and becoming one of the largest contributors to the Commonwealth Fund for Technical Cooperation, and has now joined the NDB (which is based in Shanghai but headed by an Indian for its first five years) and the AIIB. Will it strive to marshal its limited foreign assistance resources through those multilateral institutions where it has a leadership role, but which might be relatively small, or

Table 7. India's Foreign Trade, 2004–05 to 2016–17

Country/Division	2004–05 Total	2005–06 Total	2006–07 Total	2007–08 Total	2008–09 Total	2009–10 Total	2010–11 Total	2011–12 Total	2012–13 Total	2013–14 Total	2014–15 Total	2015–16 Total	2016–17 Total
Africa	17,076	21,251	29,896	35,632	47,116	45,400	59,128	80,969	86,143	79,280	83,912	65,286	60,693
South Africa	3,182	3,999	4,718	5,860	7,366	7,725	11,064	14,688	13,991	11,013	11,793	9,500	9,365
Nigeria	3,486	4,328	6,316	7,469	9,972	9,451	12,058	16,628	18,101	17,126	17,032	11,678	9,464
African countries in OPEC (ex. Nigeria)	2,000	2,483	3,624	4,285	5,721	5,423	6,918	9,540	10,385	9,826	7,458	4,340	4,161
Rest of Africa	8,409	10,441	15,237	18,018	24,057	22,800	29,088	40,113	43,666	41,315	47,630	39,768	37,702
Asia–Developing Countries (incl. SAARC)	47,550	61,432	84,975	101,753	129,932	138,901	185,770	238,589	221,677	221,777	231,418	209,420	221,766
SAARC	5,391	6,961	7,977	8,581	10,237	10,008	13,807	15,968	17,786	20,056	23,437	21,587	21,636
Afghanistan	—	201	216	291	525	589	567	637	630	689	686	835	801
Bangladesh	1,691	1,791	1,856	1,885	2,769	2,678	3,684	4,419	5,780	6,663	7,071	6,766	7,397
Bhutan	156	188	199	252	260	271	377	434	397	508	485	748	624
Maldives	48	70	72	73	132	83	132	144	129	110	157	183	207
Nepal	1,089	1,240	1,235	1,556	2,046	1,981	2,680	3,291	3,632	4,128	5,213	4,398	5,804
Pakistan	616	869	1,673	1,637	1,783	1,848	2,364	1,954	2,606	2,717	2,354	2,623	2,288
Sri Lanka	1,792	2,602	2,726	2,887	2,722	2,559	4,004	5,089	4,612	5,241	7,471	6,034	4,515

Latin American Countries	4,243	5,754	9,394	9,907	11,415	13,837	18,903	25,279	31,185	30,335	32,075	24,988	26,071
China	12,714	17,627	25,755	35,396	41,369	42,316	58,928	75,886	65,826	66,123	72,409	70,721	71,527
Russia	1,954	2,755	3,312	3,371	5,380	4,545	5,295	6,454	6,527	6,016	6,337	6,170	7,487
European Union	36,253	47,536	56,638	65,220	81,240	74,386	90,658	111,181	102,844	101,704	98,744	88,516	88,770
Canada	1,643	1,942	2,888	3,083	3,814	3,220	3,376	4,997	4,845	5,186	5,953	6,263	6,080
United States	20,767	26,808	30,602	39,885	39,414	36,465	45,338	59,213	61,388	61,535	64,266	62,101	64,416
Japan	5,363	6,542	7,458	9,186	10,793	10,336	13,716	18,501	18,520	16,275	15,509	14,500	13,600
World	195,053	252,256	312,149	377,853	488,991	467,124	620,905	795,283	791,137	764,629	758,385	643,297	659,288

Source: RBI—https://dbie.rbi.org.in/DBIE/dbie.rbi?site=home accessed on 13 July 2018; and World Integrated Trade Solutions, World Bank—https://wits.worldbank.org/ accessed on 13 July 2018

try and leverage them through large global institutions where its voice is relatively limited? There has been some cooperation with DAC donor agencies which have expressed a desire to train Afghans and Africans in India as it is more cost-effective; this has been welcomed by DPA. Some DAC agencies have also expressed interest in joint project implementation in third countries. DPA has resisted this, fearing brand equity dilution and also wanting to avoid the terms and conditions of DAC aid. There has been a DAC attempt since the Fourth High-level Forum on Aid Effectiveness (Busan, South Korea meeting) Agenda of November 2011 to launch a global partnership on aid effectiveness in which DAC donors have been trying to envelope new donors under common norms for project selection, terms and conditions, etc., particularly for the post-millennium development goals (MDG) (post-2015) development agenda. India and China have been resisting this to avoid DAC conditionalities and also avoid having the global development aid burden passed on to them in part, which would reduce the flexibility of their own programs.

Table 8. India's Outward Direct Investment Flows, 2000–2018 (U.S. $ Mn)

Year	Gross In-flows/Gross Investments	Repatriation/ Disinvest-ment	Direct Investment to India	FDI by India	Net Foreign Direct In-vestment	Net Portfolio Invest-ment	Total
2017–18	60,974	21,544	39,431	9,144	30,286	22,115	52,401
2016–17	60,220	18,005	42,215	6,603	35,612	7,612	43,224
2015–16	55,559	10,652	44,907	8,886	36,021	−4,130	31,891
2014–15	44,291	9,864	34,427	1,799	32,628	40,934	73,562
2013–14	36,047	5,284	30,763	9,199	21,564	4,822	26,386
2012–13	34,298	7,345	26,953	7,134	19,819	26,891	46,711
2011–12	46,552	13,599	32,952	10,892	22,061	17,170	39,231
2010–11	36,047	7,018	29,029	17,195	11,834	30,293	42,127
2009–10	37,746	4,637	33,109	15,143	17,966	32,396	50,362
2008–09	41,903	166	41,738	19,365	22,372	−14,030	8,342
2007–08	34,844	116	34,729	18,835	15,893	27,433	43,326
2006–07	22,826	87	22,739	15,046	7,693	7,060	14,753
2005–06	8,962	61	8,901	5,867	3,034	12,494	15,528
2004–05	6,052	65	5,987	2,274	3,713	9,287	13,000
2003–04	4,322	—	4,322	1,934	2,388	11,356	13,744
2002–03	5,095	59	5,036	1,819	3,217	944	4,161
2001–02	6,130	5	6,125	1,391	4,734	1,952	6,686
2000–01	4,031	—	4,031	759	3,272	2,590	5,862

Source: RBI, accessed July 13, 2018—https://dbie.rbi.org.in/DBIE/dbie.rbi?site=home

Table 9A. India's Outward FDI, Region-wise, 2010–2017

(U.S.D. Mn)	2010	2011	2012	2013	2014	2015	2016	2017
Continent	Total	Total	Total	Total	Total	Total	Total	Total
Africa (total)	**5,116**	**2,661**	**1,829**	**3,679**	**8,320**	**3,991**	**4,970**	**2,759**
Eastern Africa	5,098	2,582	1,762	3,466	8,223	3,890	4,899	2,695
Western Africa	—	—	—	17	30	12	18	13
Central Africa	—	—	—	0	0	0	0	0
Southern Africa	—	—	—	19	33	62	28	29
Northern Africa	18	79	67	178	36	27	25	22
Asia (total)	**7,047**	**3,891**	**4,033**	**7,469**	**9,412**	**7,816**	**8,280**	**7,985**
South Asia	1,262	260	157	173	79	140	65	191
South East Asia	4,135	2,457	1,981	4,164	6,759	5,251	6,040	5,765
Western Asia	1,449	572	1,663	2,583	2,362	2,028	1,989	1,693
Eastern Asia	201	602	232	547	212	397	180	249
Central Asia	—	—	—	1	0	0	6	87
Caribbean	—	34	55	45	28	24	13	0
EU	2,551	1,955	1,835	0	0	0	0	0
Eastern Europe	—	—	—	62	70	46	107	545
Western Europe	2,255	2,028	2,263	5,479	15,030	5,011	7,531	5,089
South America	—	—	—	51	46	102	42	86
Central America	—	—	—	38	39	17	77	62
North America	893	835	745	4,928	5,213	3,340	4,034	4,472
Oceania	—	—	—	1	3	5	9	10
Antarctica	—	—	—	0	0	0	0	0
Australia	183	313	177	141	59	103	51	60
Unspecified	1,596	666	475	39	15	39	37	47
World	**18,337**	**11,405**	**10,973**	**23,964**	**40,261**	**22,510**	**27,180**	**23,138**

Source: RBI, accessed July 13, 2018—https://dbie.rbi.org.in/DBIE/dbie.rbi?site=home

Table 9B. FDI by India to South Asian Countries, 2010–17

(U.S.D. Mn)	2010	2011	2012	2013	2014	2015	2016	2017
Country	Total	Total	Total	Total	Total	Total	Total	Total
Afghanistan	—	—	—	—	1	4	—	0
Bangladesh	—	—	—	26	10	19	9	30
Bhutan	—	—	—	6	1	0	0	0
Iran	—	—	—	—	—	—	—	—
Maldives	—	—	—	1	2	14	3	7
Nepal	—	—	—	10	3	5	2	22
Pakistan	—	—	—	—	—	—	—	—
Sri Lanka	1,262	260	157	130	63	98	52	131
Myanmar	—	—	—	16	4	1	13	50
Total	1,262	260	157	190	84	141	78	240

Source: RBI, accessed July 13, 2018—https://dbie.rbi.org.in/DBIE/dbie.rbi?site=home

India's Emerging Trade and Investment Relationships: Correlation with Development Partnership?

India's foreign assistance policy does not seem to be related to trade and investment relationships as far as its major thrust, South Asia, is concerned. Table 7 gives India's total trade with various regions and countries from 2004–05 to 2016–17 including with the countries of South Asia.

India's gross merchandize trade increased during the period of the new assistance policy from 23 percent of GDP in 2004–05 to 43 percent in 2011–12 before declining to 29 percent in 2016–17, while its exports increased from 10 percent to 17 percent before declining to 11 percent of GDP for the same years, indicating a rapidly globalizing economy even after the global financial crisis of 2008.[7] India's trade with the countries of the South Asian region, a major focus of Indian assistance with 47 percent of Exim Bank credit, amounts to only 3.3 percent of its overall trade in 2016–17, up from 2.8 percent in 2004–05, and only 7 percent of its exports in 2016–17, from only 5.5 percent in 2004–05. India's trade with, and exports to, Afghanistan, remain tiny at 0.14 percent and 0.2 percent, respectively, as at 2016–17. Likewise, India's trade with, and exports to, Myanmar remain tiny at 0.24 percent and 0.36 percent, respectively, as at 2016–17.

India's outward private investment flows increased steadily, from a very low base, over 2001–02 to 2017–18, rising from $759 m to over $19 bn in 2008–09 then down to $9.1 bn in 2017–18, totaling $177.77 bn over the period (Table 8). As Table 9A shows, the bulk of Indian outward FDI since 2010 has gone to developed Western Europe ($44.7 bn) and North America ($24.5 bn), and to Southeast Asia (mainly, developed Singapore) ($36.6 bn), oil-rich West Asia ($14.3 bn), resource-rich South America, and not to the main aided regions with the sole exception of Eastern Africa. Private investment flows to South Asia of $2.33 bn (Table 9B) are very small (just over 1 percent of all outward FDIs over 2010–17), although they are significant from the host country's point of view in the cases of Bhutan, Nepal, and Sri Lanka.[8] They are practically nonexistent for Afghanistan, Myanmar, Nepal, and Bangladesh, all recipients of a significant chunk of Indian assistance since 2004–05.

As far as Africa is concerned, trade, exports, and imports show the following pattern over the past few years (2013–17). For sub-Saharan (non-Arab) Africa as a whole, India's trade from that continent has decreased from 9.2 percent to 8.1 percent of its total trade, exports decreased from 10.3 percent to 8.3 percent, and imports from 8.5 percent to 8.1 percent.[9] As of 2016–17, total trade with Africa was about $61 bn, less than trade with China at $71 bn. If we look at Africa sub-regionally and

country-wise in 2017, we see that $20 bn trade is with West Africa and $13 bn with Southern Africa out of a total of $61 bn. This is due to the dominant shares of just two countries in Indo-African trade—Nigeria with $9.46 bn and South Africa with $9.37 bn, totaling $18.83 bn. This is due to large imports from these energy- and resource-rich countries, India's trade profile with these two countries being dominated by imports. However, out of total assistance to Africa, these two countries are not at all dominant in the assistance profile, the overwhelming bulk of the assistance going to less developed or less resource-rich countries.

Outward FDI and assistance are also not correlated at all with respect to Africa except for East Africa ($32.62 bn, almost 98% of the total to Africa of $33.33 bn), a somewhat suspect figure which needs to be further investigated, the rest of Africa getting under 2 percent of Indian FDI commitments.

Program Evolution and Motivations: Politico-Security Concerns in India's Assistance

If trade and investment relations have not been the prime drivers what have been the motivations behind India's development partnership program? To situate the program in its politico-security and economic context, we situate it in the evolution of India's foreign policy with respect to the major regions of the program's concentration, viz., South Asia, Afghanistan, Myanmar, and the African continent, in this section, based on detailed confidential interviews.[10]

Bhutan

The assistance relationship with Bhutan, along with Nepal, is the oldest and most consistent. India's relations with Bhutan have been governed by the India–Bhutan Treaty of August 8, 1949, and the updated and revised treaty called the India–Bhutan Friendship Treaty signed in February 2007, by which India *de facto* controlled its foreign relations, a carry-forward of the situation before Indian independence. Bhutan is a monarchy that inherited and continued its strategic status after India's independence as a Himalayan buffer state between India and China, and still does not have formal diplomatic relations with China, although relations are growing despite an unresolved border. India now accounts for 80 percent of Bhutan's imports and 94 percent of its exports, although the former figure is expected to be rapidly reduced by Bhutan's growing relations with China. Bhutan's export earnings are overwhelmingly from its export of hydroelectric power to India. India is the largest trade and development partner of Bhutan. Bhutan along with Nepal became a priority country after the October–November 1962 Sino–Indian border war. Assistance to Bhutan has been integrated into India's planning process and a number of grants are made under the head of Plan grants by the MEA.

After the shift in India's overall assistance policy from 2004, and stepped-up border management and security cooperation by Bhutan in De-

cember 2003–January 2004 in taking action against Indian insurgent groups (United Liberation Front of Assam) holed up in Bhutan, Bhutan's Ninth Plan assistance was reviewed. In March 2004, an Indo-Bhutan Group on Border Security and Management was established. The subsequent stepping up of assistance has to be seen in this context.

In 2005, it was decided to renew the bilateral Trade, Commerce and Transit Agreement for another 10 years, and an umbrella agreement on power projects in Bhutan was finalized. In 2008, on the occasion of the centenary of the Wangchuck dynasty and the coronation of the fifth king, India agreed to double its assistance to Bhutan's 10th five-year plan (over the ninth plan) to Rs. 34,000 m ($700 m). This would consist of Rs. 20,000 m ($400 m) for 65 projects, mostly small development projects (SDPs), first introduced in Nepal and then in Bhutan, to be spread all over Bhutan. In March 2009, an Empowered Joint Group on Hydroelectric Power Development in Bhutan met to discuss the development of 10,000 MW of hydropower generation in Bhutan for export to India by 2020. Implementation agreements were signed later, indicating growing economic integration with India.

Nepal

Nepal, another Himalayan buffer state between India and China, is vital for India's border security, particularly after the 1962 border war with China. The 1,850 kilometer Indo-Nepal border is a porous one with free movement of people. Nepal is a weak and unstable multi-party democracy that has been wracked by a Maoist insurgency since the mid-1990s. On February 1, 2005, the government was dissolved as the Maoist insurgency spread, triggering talks of the Joint Working Group on Border Management and the India–Nepal Bilateral Consultative Group on Security Issues. The Joint Committee on Water Resources also met in 2004–05, and an MOU was signed on an oil pipeline, and rail service commenced in July 2004.

The SDP program is central to India's assistance to Nepal. It was introduced in 2003, and by 2010–11, there were 400 projects in all 75 districts of Nepal. The aim is to spread the impact of assistance and also local awareness of it in the host country. In 2011–12, an Indo-Nepal Bilateral Investment Promotion and Protection Agreement (BIPPA) and a Double Taxation Avoidance Agreement were signed. More recently, Indian Prime Minister Modi announced a \$1 bn credit line for hydropower, irrigation, and infrastructure in August 2014.

Over the entire period since the Emergency of 2005, India helped to politically stabilize Nepal, seen as vital for Indian security, by encouraging peace talks and the restoration of democracy and building up of a constitutional development process in Nepal at Nepal's invitation. Nepal agreed that it would not allow anti-India insurgent activities. Assistance to Nepal has to be placed in this context along with the fact that India now accounts for 60 percent of Nepal's foreign trade and 44 percent of its

inward FDI, and India is the largest assistance provider and source of tourists. However, India faces stiff competition from China in economic assistance for political influence and Nepal has been adroitly playing the two off against each other.

Bangladesh

India–Bangladesh relations after the latter's independence in 1972 were governed by the 25-year India–Bangladesh Friendship Treaty, which was allowed to lapse in 1997 by the then Awami League government of Sheikh Hasina Wazed despite the signing of the watershed Indo-Bangladesh Ganga Waters Treaty in December 1996 which addressed Bangladesh's long-standing demands on river water-sharing.[11] The 1972 Treaty provided that neither country would harm the security of the other. The lapsing of this treaty removed this security feature from the Indian point of view, and in fact, since then India has suspected Bangladesh, particularly during the Bangladesh National Party government of 2001–06, of conniving with terrorist activities directed against India by nonstate actors. Despite starting on a promising note, relations have been bedeviled by a number of issues including an unresolved "ragged" boundary, illegal immigration of Bangladeshis into India, sharing of waters of 54 common rivers, primarily the Ganges, the operation of anti-Indian insurgent, and terrorist groups from Bangladesh. Hence, Bangladesh is a neighbor with whom India's relations are sensitive. Assistance to Bangladesh has to be seen in this context.

Talks in 2004–05 between the new UPA government in India and the Bangladesh government included the biannual Director-General-level talks between the two border guard forces, the issue of insurgent and radical Islamist groups, sharing of the Teesta river waters, illegal immigration, trade, investment and the possible Myanmar–Bangladesh–India gas pipeline, and the annual meeting of the Joint Rivers Commission. The year 2006–07 saw a revised Trade Agreement. The Joint Boundary Working Group met after a gap of four years and discussed the Land Boundary Agreement of 1974. An Indo-Bangladesh Chamber of Commerce and Industry was inaugurated in 2007–08 and a trial run of the Kolkata (Calcutta)–Dhaka passenger train took place, leading to the start of rail services the next year. A trade agreement and a BIPPA were signed in February 2009.

The Grand Alliance (GA) government led by the Awami League of Sheikh Hasina Wazed was formed in January 2009 and took steps to improve relations with India. She visited India in January 2010, following which an LOC of $1 bn for infrastructure projects, including railways, was signed in August, as was a 35-year power transmission agreement. Indian prime minister Manmohan Singh visited Bangladesh in September 2011 resulting in the Land Boundary Demarcation Agreement, an increase in the annual duty-free export quota of garments to India, a joint venture agreement for the 1,320 MW Khulna power plant, and increased defense cooperation and an increased number of ITEC and Colombo Plan training

slots. More recently, Prime Minister Modi announced an additional $2 bn credit line focused on infrastructure in his 2015 visit, which also saw the resolution of the long-festering boundary issue. The stepping up of assistance is clearly linked to the cooperative attitude of the GA government and the perceived importance of its stability for Indian security. However, Indo-Bangladesh trade remains sluggish, with India accounting for only 13 percent of Bangladesh's imports, in sharp contrast to dominating the imports of landlocked Nepal and Bhutan.

Sri Lanka

Sri Lanka, which was in the throes of a long-drawn out separatist war over 1983–2009 between the government and the Liberation Tigers of Tamil Eelam (LTTE), a separatist guerilla group of the hitherto discriminated-against Tamils of the North and East of the island, signed a free trade agreement with India in 1998, operational from 2000, called the India–Sri Lanka Free Trade Agreement. This gradually liberalized trade ahead of the South Asian regional trade liberalization process and also had the effect of encouraging Indian investment in Sri Lanka to take advantage of lower tariffs on raw materials, and consequent export of products back to India. The free trade agreement and the domestic peace process between the Tamil rebels and the government, marked by the Ceasefire Agreement of 2002, led to an improvement of Indo-Sri Lanka relations, and Sri Lanka supported India's bid for a permanent UNSC seat. There were the beginnings of moves to upgrade the FTA to a Comprehensive Economic Partnership Agreement (CEPA). India had become the biggest FDI source by 2004 and the fourth largest cumulatively.

In November 2005, Mahinda Rajapakse was elected president of Sri Lanka and visited India in December. India stressed the importance of political dialog and pressed its view that there was no military solution, and offered to share its constitutional experience. By 2007, India became the largest single source of tourists, the largest single source of imports and third largest destination for Sri Lankan exports. The civil war ended in May 2009 with the elimination of the LTTE, and President Rajapakse was re-elected in January 2010. India stressed the importance of reconciliation and a devolution-based political solution to the conflict, and gave assistance for relief and rehabilitation of the internal refugees.

India opened two new consulates-general, resumed ferry services, renewed the MOU on SDPs, signed a new MOU on Interconnection of Electricity Grids, increased defense cooperation focused on army and navy chief visits and training, an LOC of $415 m for the Northern Railway line, a de-mining team, a package for relief and rehabilitation and a commitment to build 50,000 houses for the internally displaced persons in the Northern, Eastern, and Central provinces. Sri Lanka assured India that political proposals for devolution of power building on the 13th Amendment to its constitution would be discussed with the Tam-il leadership but has dragged its feet even under the new government that took power in 2015. India remained the largest trade partner, largest FDI, and tourist source, and sees engagement as vital for leverage. Assistance is part of this engagement and leverage on both internal reform and for providing an incentive to maintain a distance from a China that has emerged as the largest donor to Sri Lanka since the end of the civil war in 2009. India has stepped up its aid since then in response to the geopolitical competition for influence from China, signified most dramatically in Sri Lanka giving the southern Hambantota port, overlooking the main Indian Ocean sea lanes, to China on a 99-year lease in 2017.

Afghanistan

Afghanistan has emerged as one of the largest single-country assistance programs for India. The political background to this is as follows, in brief. After the 9/11 attacks in the United States, and the subsequent invasion, overthrow of the Taliban regime and occupation of Afghanistan by U.S.-led NATO forces in late 2001, and the Bonn Agreement of December 2001, India made assistance commitments to the post-war reconstruction of Afghanistan. This began with $100 m in January 2002 at the Tokyo Donors Conference. This needs to be seen in light of the erstwhile Taliban regime's complicity in the hijack of an Indian aircraft in December 1999 and its closeness to the Pakistani military. It was in India's security interests to stabilize a moderate and democratic alternative in Afghanistan.

Indian assistance was focused on three major infrastructure projects: (i) upgradation of the Zaranj–Delaram highway of 218 kilometers; (ii) the Salma Dam project in Herat province in the west; (iii) the 220 kV double circuit transmission line from Pul-e-Khomri to Kabul, and the 220/110/20 kV substation at Chimtala to bring power from Uzbekistan to Kabul, all completed by 2010.

Apart from this, India undertook to build the new Afghan parliament building, contributed to the Afghan Reconstruction Fund, and to a broad SDP program, which paralleled similar SDP programs that were in existence in Bhutan and Nepal, including assistance in the agriculture, education, healthcare, and medical sciences areas.

In 2006–07, the security situation worsened with increasing attacks by the Taliban insurgents through most of the country. Two Indians working in the country were killed. MOUs in rural development and education were signed, and India participated in the November 2006 second Regional Economic Cooperation Conference in Afghanistan and the parallel Regional Business Conference on Afghanistan hosted by the Federation of Indian Chambers of Commerce and Industry (FICCI), the Confederation of Indian Industry (CII), and the Associated Chambers of Commerce and Industry (Assocham). Cumulative Indian assistance rose to $750 m by 2006–07. The year saw new project commitments like expansion of TV coverage, and the training of Afghan diplomats in the Foreign Service Training Institute in Delhi. About a thousand training slots were given to Afghans in the ITEC program. India supported the admission of Afghanistan to the South Asian Association for Regional Cooperation (SAARC) at the 14th SAARC summit in Delhi in April 2007 as its eighth member.

India welcomed the Obama speech of December 2009 on strengthening the Afghan government and security forces as preparation to the eventual U.S. drawdown and pullout, and participated in the UN International Conference on Afghanistan in London in January 2010. This was a prelude to the stepping up of India's security cooperation with Afghanistan from the next year. President Karzai's visit in October 2011 resulted in an Agreement on Strategic Partnership, the first such with any country for Afghanistan. This included political and security cooperation, and an MOU on hydrocarbons and minerals. An additional $500 m of assistance was announced during the visit taking the cumulative total assistance by then to $2 bn.

India's assistance strategy, to some extent, mirrors its assistance experience in countries like Bhutan and Nepal in that it focused not just on a few major high-profile projects but on a range of widespread small projects and capacity building by offering scholarships to students and trainees, and thereby building long-term human contacts.

India's assistance strategy in Afghanistan is geared to supporting and stabilizing the Afghan government in both political and economic terms to secure India's perceived long-term security interests, against a possible future re-conquest of the country by the Taliban operating with covert backing from Pakistan. In recent years, China too has increased its level of activity in Afghanistan, something not to India's comfort given the *de facto* Pakistan–China alliance.

Myanmar

Myanmar is India's neighbor, bordering four northeastern Indian states, with a 1,650 kilometer border, and an ethnic Naga insurgency that overlaps that border. It also has about 400,000 people of Indian origin, mostly very poor. India has followed a policy of engagement with the military regime in Myanmar from the mid-1990s, its policy being based on cultivating Myanmar to prevent it from going entirely into the hands of China politically and to gain Myanmar's cooperation in tackling the Naga insurgency, de-prioritizing democracy, and the Indian minority. In return, Myanmar supported India's bid for UNSC permanent membership and has been cooperative on the Naga insurgency issue. Annual foreign office consultations began in 1995.[12]

Assistance to Myanmar increased gradually over the past decade. An MOU for the Chindwin hydroelectric project was signed in 2004–05, and one on the India–Myanmar–Thailand trilateral highway project following the Myanmar foreign minister's visit in July 2004. This was followed by MOUs on railways and energy cooperation *inter*

alia a possible Myanmar–Bangladesh–India gas pipeline. The idea was to work toward the integration of India's northeastern states with Myanmar and further afield with booming Southeast Asia and Southwest China.

A BCIM group (Bangladesh–China–India–Myanmar) cooperation meeting was held in March 2006. A Double Taxation Avoidance Agreement and a BIPPA were signed in 2008–09. Emergency humanitarian assistance was rushed to Myanmar following Cyclone Nargis in May 2008.

Cooperation was significantly stepped up in 2010–11, mainly LOCs for oil and gas, power, railways, and highways. A delegation from Northeastern India visited Myanmar to promote subregional cooperation. The Myanmar president Thein Sein visited India in October 2011 (coincidentally coinciding with Afghan President Karzai's visit), an LOC of $500 m was extended and a target was set for $3 bn in trade by 2015. The stepping up of assistance is part of a strategy to support Myanmar's democratization and relative shift away from dependence on China.

Africa

Indian foreign policy has traditionally supported decolonization, and opposed racism and apartheid. India had been offering training and expertise to Africa under the ITEC program since the 1960s. In the period of the 1990s and in the twenty-first century, in the context of the liberalization and faster growth of India's economy, the end of apartheid in South Africa in 1994, the liberalization and faster growth of African economies since 2002, Indian policy has come to pay greater attention to Africa. At the start of India's new foreign assistance policy from 2004 to 2005 onwards, the Indian president addressed the Pan-African Parliament in 2004, India was part of UN Peacekeeping Forces in four countries, and most of Africa had endorsed India's candidature for a permanent UNSC seat.

In 2004, India declared its intent to build a fiber-optic E-connectivity network for Africa. There was also close cooperation with the ECOWAS group of West African states (established 1975). In 2005, India engaged with COMESA (Common Market for Eastern and Southern Africa, established 1994) based on an India-COMESA MOU. An India–Africa Conclave was held in Delhi in March 2005, and the SADC-India Forum was approved by the (14 nations) SADC (Southern Africa Development Community, established 1992) Council of Ministers. The TEAM-9 Initiative (India plus eight West African countries) was launched at the margins of the UN General Assembly in New York in September 2005 and a $500 m LOC offered to TEAM-9. An LOC of $200 m was extended to several countries for execution of projects and purchase of equipment under the New Partnership for African Development (NEPAD). India joined the African Capacity Building Foundation (based in Harare) as a full member. Four thousand ITEC and SCAAP slots were allotted to Africa, spanning 39 institutions in India.

A landmark event in India's assistance policy to Africa was the India–Africa Forum Summit held on April 2008 in Delhi. It ended with the Delhi Declaration, a new architecture and framework for Africa-India cooperation, and a doubling of LOCs to Africa to $5.4 bn over the next five years (2008–13), concentrated in agriculture and food, small and medium enterprises, irrigation, infrastructure, IT, energy, and pharmaceuticals. Scholarships were doubled, and a Duty Free Tariff Preference scheme for access to products from African LDCs was initiated. A second India-Africa Forum Summit was held in 2011 and a third in 2015, both marked by step-ups of assistance.

Four Indo-African institutions were established as part of the follow-up to the India-African Forum Summit. These were the India–Africa Institute of Foreign Trade, India-Africa Diamond Institute, India-Africa Institute of Educational Planning and Administration, and the India-Africa Institute of Information Technology.

The Duty Free Tariff Preference scheme was offered to 33 African Least Developed Countries, of which 18 acceded to it. The Pan-African E-network was implemented in 34 out of 47 states in 2010–11.

In May 2011, the second Africa-India Forum Summit was held in Addis Ababa, resulting in the Addis Ababa Declaration and Africa–India Framework for Enhanced Cooperation, another step-up in the level of cooperation. The Declaration was a political document covering UN reform, WTO, climate change, and terrorism among other things.

The second meeting between India and African Regional Economic Communities was held in November 2011. India has MOUs with four such entities—COMESA, ECOWAS, EC-CAS (Economic Community of Central African States, established 1985), and SADC. South Africa joined the BRIC grouping, making it BRICS, in April 2011 and the fifth IBSA summit was held in Pretoria. Africa is the second largest recipient ($9.23 bn) among regions (after South Asia) of the $22.52 bn in LOCs extended by India till June 2018.

India's attractiveness to Africa lies in its ability to produce soft infrastructure like IT goods and services and pharmaceutical products relatively cheaply and some see it as offering an alternative to Chinese assistance and trade (Naidu 2008). Access to African oil and gas resources for long-term energy security and as an alternative to the volatile Middle East also remains a goal of India's Africa policy (Naidu 2008). Assistance also complements the growing footprint of Indian companies in Africa and helps promote trade and investment, including in minerals.

Development assistance to Africa is not a case of immediate economic benefits or of short-term security competition with China but more of investment in long-term relationship-building with a resource-rich continent with close to 50 UN General Assembly votes that promises to be increasingly important in the future in both economic and political terms. All African countries have been visited by Indian ministers during the Modi government's tenure and Indian Ocean maritime security cooperation has also been discussed with several African states.[13]

Discernible Patterns

Among the major recipients of Indian assistance, the following patterns are discernible:

First, in the cases of Bhutan and Nepal, India bulks large in their trade, inward investment, and tourism profiles, while they are of marginal significance in India's trade and outward investment profile. They matter to India's security calculations in a major way as they are neighbors with porous borders and buffer states between India and China. Hence, India's assistance to them is primarily motivated by political and security considerations but is important to the recipients in economic terms. An important point here is that India's assistance is widely distributed in the form of a large number of small projects, thus maximizing popular awareness and impact. Also that India being the principal destination for higher studies and training creates an alumni network in both countries. India's assistance is one of long-term commitment as signified by the fact that it comes from its Plan budget as well as Non-Plan budget for decades.

Second, Bangladesh and Sri Lanka, which are neighbors in which India perceives competition for diplomatic influence from Pakistan and China, are both insignificant to India's trade and outward investment profile but of considerable importance to the recipients' trade, inward investment, remittances (for Bangladesh), and tourism (for Sri Lanka) profile. In both cases, Indian assistance is fairly recent, becoming significant over the past half-decade, and relatively concentrated in large LOC. Scholarships and training are significant in both cases.

Third, Afghanistan and Myanmar are again recent cases of assistance, motivated primarily by political and security considerations with perceived competition for political influence from Pakistan and China, respectively. In both cases, the recipient country is of marginal economic but major geopolitical significance to India, although both can be of significance for India's natural resource needs in the future. This is because if the democratically elected Afghan government is not stabilized, and if there is a Pakistani-backed Taliban takeover after an eventual U.S. pullout, then a regime backing terrorism against India might get entrenched in Kabul. Likewise, a Myanmar overwhelmingly dependent on China is not in India's security interests, given the growing Chinese presence in the Indian Ocean. India does not bulk large in Afghanistan's or Myanmar's trade and inward investment. The pattern of assistance is one of large LOCs rather than small projects, although this is beginning to happen in Afghanistan, where scholarships and training are also significant.

Fourth, in the case of Africa, assistance again is recent in its growth,

particularly after the India–Africa summits of 2008, 2011, and 2015. It consists of 158 of 227 operative LoCs, with an average worth of $58 m, to 36 countries and the ECOWAS Bank of Investment spread across the continent, and is concentrated in fairly large to medium projects in infrastructure and agriculture, although scholarships and training are important. Within Africa, there has been a shift of Indian assistance from Eastern and Southern Africa to West Africa, recognized to be energy- and mineral-rich. However, in 2016–17 as noted earlier, $18.83 bn of the $61 trade was with Nigeria and South Africa only, and these are not where the LOCs go. Assistance is not driven by immediate trade and resource considerations but by long-term relationship-building, plus close to 50 UN General Assembly votes factored in.

Fifth, comparing the Modi government with the previous Manmohan Singh government, one sees more continuity than change and a stepping up of LOCs from the Exim Bank as India's economic capacity increases. The major areas of focus remain South Asia and Africa as before. However, India now faces increased economic and political competition from China in its South Asian neighborhood with all countries other than India having signed up for the Belt and Road Initiative including its maritime component, and China having gained influence in Nepal, Sri Lanka, and the Maldives during the tenure of the Modi government.

An Overall Assessment

Four major points emerge from an overall assessment of the Indian development partnership program.

First, India eschews terms like aid and donor, and prefers to use the term "development partner" as a fellow developing country and DAC aid recipient. It is only with the formation of the DPA, that India's "demand-driven" and politically punctuated assistance can be said to have acquired the character of a program. As the amounts increased, it gradually acquired the character of a program in two shifts—the shift to LOCs through the Exim Bank from 2004, and the formation of the DPA as an implementation agency in 2012.

Second, while the purpose of partnership is admittedly political, it is meant to cultivate goodwill toward India and long-term relationships rather than immediate payoffs, either political or economic, particularly in the case of Africa.

Third, the MEA considers the ITEC program the most cost-effective and the one that had yielded the best returns in terms of long-term goodwill because it trains key personnel in India and builds long-term human relationships. These are considered important as money alone is not enough to buy influence. India, because of English language education, is seen to have a comparative advantage in education and training of developing country personnel.

Fourth, there is no clear economic development philosophy or macroeconomic policy prescription that emerges from a scrutiny of the development partnership program. The basic philosophy seems to be seen as a fellow developing country partner that fits in with what the recipient wants except that the assistance is largely tied to India-sourced supplies, similar in this respect to early-stage Western aid. However, if the development partnership program acquires a more programmatic rather than a jerky, politically punctuated, and *ad hoc* character, one might expect a prescriptive development strategy to emerge over time either on its own or in learning/partnering processes with established Western aid programs or in the context of new, South-led lending institutions like the NDB and the AIIB. However, this might possibly be in tension with the explicit policy position at present that the development program is to serve national, that is, foreign policy interests, although these have been seen so far in a long-term perspective.

Overall, India appears to have operated on the realist assumptions of power politics and interest-orientation in its assistance policies, particularly with its neighbors, and especially energy security as regards Africa, as argued by Six (2009) and Fuchs and Vadlamannati (2013), and in line with the earlier work on developed donor motivations by Alesina and Dollar (2000). However, as we said earlier, the Indian focus is on the long run more than for immediate gains. India's partnership relationships with Bhutan, Nepal, Bangladesh, and Sri Lanka, and with Afghanistan and Myanmar, remain essentially determined by the objective of having its neighbors favorably inclined toward India. However, assistance seems to be more a defensive than a coercive or control strategy, to incentivize bandwagoning toward India or at least not incline toward India's geopolitical competitors, faced with competition in recent years from a China that can deploy much greater resources in development assistance. From a practitioner's standpoint, as emphasized in interviews, the Indian program is about building long-term relationships and not about immediate benefit. This is particularly the case in South Asia but also applies to Africa.

References

Agrawal, S. 2007. "Emerging Donors in International Development Assistance: The India Case." IDRC. Accessed April 2, 2016. http://www.idrc.ca/EN/Documents/Case-of-India.pdf.

Alesina, A., and D. Dollar. 2000. "Who Gives Foreign Aid to Whom and Why?." *Journal of Economic Growth* 5 (1): 33-63.

Brautigam, D. 2009. *The Dragon's Gift: The Real Story of China in Africa*. Oxford: Oxford University Press.

Chanana, D. 2009. "India as an Emerging Donor." *Economic and Political Weekly* 44 (12): 11-14.

Chaturvedi, S. 2008. "Emerging Patterns in Architecture for Management of Economic Assistance and Development Cooperation: Implications and Challenges for India." *RIS-Discussion Paper, 139*, accessed April 2, 2016. http://www.ris.org.in.

Chaturvedi, S. 2012a. "India and Development Cooperation: Expressing Southern Solidarity." In *Development Cooperation and Emerging Powers*, edited by S. Chaturvedi, T. Fues, and E. Sidoropoulos, 169-89. London: Zed Books.

Chaturvedi, S. 2012b. "India's Development Partnership: Key Policy Shifts and Institutional Evolution." *Cambridge Review of International Affairs* 25 (4): 557-77.

Chin, G.T., and B.M. Frolic. 2007. "Emerging Donors in International Development Assistance: The China Case." IDRC. Accessed April 2, 2016. http://www.idrc.ca/EN/Documents/Case-of-China.pdf.

De Renzio, P., and J. Seifert. 2014. "South–South Cooperation and the Future of Development Assistance: Mapping Actors and Options." *Third World Quarterly* 35 (10): 1860-75.

Duclos, V. 2012. "Building Capacities: The Resurgence of Indo-African Techno-economic Cooperation." *India Review* 11 (4): 209-25.

Egreteau, R. 2011. "A Passage to Burma? India, Development, and the Democratization in Myanmar." *Contemporary Politics* 17 (4): 467-86.

Fuchs, A., and K.C. Vadlamannati.

2013. "The Needy Donor: An Empirical Analysis of India's Aid Motives." *World Development* 44: 110-28.

Govt. of India. 2015. "Government of India Portal on Development Assistance." Accessed April 2, 2016. http://www.externalassistance.gov.in/portal/.

Gu, J., Y. Chen, and W. Haibin. 2016. "China on the Move: The New "Silk Road" to International Development Cooperation?." In *The BRICS in International Development*, edited by J. Gu, A. Shankland, and A. Chenoy, London: Palgrave Macmillan.

Kabir, M.H. 2011. "Obstacles to Bangladesh–India Cooperation: An International Relations Theory Perspective." In *International Relations Theory and South Asia: Security, Political Economy, Domestic Politics, Identities and Images*, vol. 1, edited by E. Sridharan, pp. 329-68. New Delhi: Oxford University Press.

Kragelund, P. 2010. "India's African Engagement." Real Instituto Elcano. Accessed April 2, 2016. http://www.realinstituoelcano.org.

Lagerkvist, J. 2009. "Chinese Eyes on Africa: Authoritarian Flexibility versus Democratic Governance." *Journal of Contemporary African Studies* 27 (2): 119-34.

Lancaster, C. 2007. "The Chinese Aid System." Center for Global Development. Accessed April 2, 2016. http://www.cgdev.org.

Manning, R. 2006. "Will 'Emerging Donors' Change the Face of International Cooperation?." *Development Policy Review* 24 (4): 371-85.

Ministry of External Affairs, India. *Annual Reports*, 1991-92 to 2014-15. Accessed December 15, 2015. http://www.mea.gov.in/annual-reports.htm?57/Annual_Reports.

Ministry of Finance, India. *Economic Survey*, 1984-85 to 2014-15. Accessed December 15, 2015. http://finmin.nic.in/the_ministry/dept_eco_affairs/dea.asp.

Ministry of Finance India. *Annual Budget*, 1991-92 to 2014-15. Accessed December 20, 2015. http://indiabudget.nic.in/glance.asp.

Mullen, R.D. 2012. "India Flexes Its Foreign Aid Muscle." *Current History* 111 (744): 154-56.

Mullen, R.D. 2013. "Holding Back on Soft Power." *Indian Express*, March 4.

Naidu, S. 2008. "India's Growing African Strategy." *Review of African Political Economy* 35 (115): 116-28.

Naim, M. 2007. "Rogue Aid." *Foreign Policy* 159 (March–April): 95-96.

Paulo, S., and H. Reisen. 2010. "Eastern Donors and Western Soft Law: Towards and DAC Donor Peer Review of China and India?." *Development Policy Review* 28 (5): 535-52.

People's Republic of China. 2011.

"China's Foreign Aid." Information Office of the State Council, People's Republic of China.

Price, G. 2005. "Diversity in Donorship: The Changing Landscape of Official Humanitarian Aid: India's Official Aid Programme." Overseas Development Institute. Accessed April 2, 2016. http://www.odi.org.

Reilly, J. 2012. "A Norm-Taker or Norm-Maker? Chinese Aid in Southeast Asia." *Journal of Contemporary China* 21 (73): 71-91.

Reserve Bank of India. 2015. "Database on the Indian Economy." Accessed December 20, 2015. http://dbie.rbi.org.in/DBIE/dbie.rbi?site=statistics.

Six, C. 2009. "The Rise of Postcolonial States as Donors: A Challenge to the Development Paradigm?." *Third World Quarterly* 30 (6): 1103-21.

Walz, J., and V. Ramachandran. 2011. "Brave New World: A Literature Review of Emerging Donors and the Changing Nature of Foreign Assistance." *CGD Working Paper 273*. Accessed April 2, 2016, 1-23. http://www.cgdev.org/content/publications/detail/1425691.

Woods, N. 2008. "Whose Aid? Whose Influence? China, Emerging Donors and the Silent Revolution in Development Assistance." *International Affair* 84 (6): 1205-21.

Notes

1   Accessed August 4, 2018. https://stats.oecd.org/index.aspx?lang=en.

2   See Chaturvedi (2012a, 2012b, 171-77) for a historical account until the 2000s.

3   Source: Accessed December 15, 2015. http://finmin.nic.in/the_ministry/dept_eco_affairs/cie2sec/cie2sec_index.asp.

4   See note 3.

5   "Ministry of External Affairs." *Annual Report 2017-18*, 193-94.

6   In fact, the former head of the DPA, Ambassador P.S. Raghavan was explicit that aid by a low-income country like India could only be justified if it was clearly linked to foreign policy needs. Interview with Ambassador P.S. Raghavan, March 8, 2013, New Delhi.

7   See the Indian Ministry of Commerce database: http://commerce.nic.in/eidb/iecnttopnq.asp and the Reserve Bank of India database: http://dbie.rbi.org.in/DBIE/dbie.rbi?site=statistics and World Integrated Trade Solutions, World Bank—https://wits.worldbank.org/ for the figures in this section. Accessed on August 4, 2018.

8   Ministry of External Affairs, *Annual Reports*, various years, pages for these countries.

9   World Integrated Trade Solutions, World Bank—accessed August 3, 2018. https://wits.worldbank.org/

10   All facts and figures in the country accounts in this section are from Indian Ministry of External Affairs, *Annual Reports*, various years, and anonymous conversations with nine senior Indian diplomats with experience of the various countries and regions covered, including two former heads of the DPA, and a former chairman and managing director of the Exim Bank of India, besides the foregoing sections.

11   See Kabir (2011) for a comprehensive overview of Indo-Bangladesh relations.

12   See Egreteau (2011) for an account of contemporary India–Myanmar relations.

13   Ministry of External Affairs, *Annual Report 2017-18*, xi-xii.

Acknowledgments

The authors acknowledge the financial support from the International Development Research Centre (IDRC), Ottawa, Canada. The authors are solely responsible for the facts, figures, and interpretations in this article.

Parameters of Successful Wastewater Reuse in Urban India

Kelly D. Alley

Auburn University, alleykd@auburn.edu *(corresponding author)*[1]

Nutan Maurya

South Asian University, nutanmaurya@gmail.com

Sukanya Das

TERI University, sukanya.das@terisas.ac.in

Research for this article was supported by the National Science Foundation, Cultural Anthropology Program, Award #1628014. The authors thank the reviewers for their helpful feedback.

ABSTRACT

Studies of surface and groundwater in India show that dry season water availability will continue to decline over the next half-century, a challenge that will face many areas and countries around the globe. The need to develop wastewater recycling schemes is critical to improving conditions of water supply and ensuring the survival of agriculture and human consumption, as well as industrial production. The need for wastewater recycling is pushing communities, governments, and businesses to discuss, experiment with, and pilot projects using decentralized methods. This paper introduces four cases of wastewater recycling that are considered "success" stories and identifies the key parameters that enable these systems to function. The parameters pertain to human dimensions involving historical, institutional, regulatory, policy, and economic conditions and innovations. We then use these labels as heuristics for models of success in Indian conditions.

Keywords: wastewater, water reuse, recycling, closed loop, hydrosocial cycle, National Green Tribunal, flexibat, India

Resumen

Los estudios de aguas superficiales y subterráneas en India muestran que la disponibilidad de agua en la estación seca continuará disminuyendo durante el próximo medio siglo, un desafío que enfrentarán muchas áreas y países en todo el mundo. La necesidad de desarrollar esquemas de reciclaje de agua residual es crítica para mejorar las condiciones de suministro de agua y asegurar la supervivencia de la agricultura, el consumo humano y la producción industrial. La necesidad de reciclar aguas residuales está impulsando a las comunidades, gobiernos y negocios a discutir y experimentar con proyectos que utilizan métodos descentralizados. Este documento presenta cuatro casos de reciclaje de aguas residuales que son considerados "éxitosos" e identifica los parámetros clave que le permiten funcionar a estos sistemas. Los parámetros tienen que ver con las dimensiones que involucran condiciones históricas, institucionales, regulatorias, políticas y económicas y también innovaciones. Luego usamos estas etiquetas como heurísticas para modelos de éxito en condiciones indias.

Palabras clave: aguas residuales, reutilización del agua, reciclaje, ciclo cerrado, ciclo hidrosocial, National Green Tribunal, flexibat, India

摘要

有关印度地表水和地下水的研究表明，干旱季节水资源的可获取性将在下半个世纪内持续下降，全球许多地区和国家都将面临这一挑战。发展废水回用计划之需对于提高水供应、保障农业和人类消费而言至关重要，对工业生产而言也是如此。废水回用之需正在推动各社区、政府和公司就分散方法的使用对试点项目进行探讨和实验。本文介绍了四个被认为是成功案例的废水回用实例，同时识别了让这些废水回用系统得以运作的关键参数。参数所涉及的维度包括历史、制度、监管、政策和经济形势、以及创新。笔者之后将这些标签 作为启发式方法，探索印度形势的成功模式。

关键词：废水，废水回用，再循环，闭合环路，社会水循环，印度国家绿色法庭，flexibat，印度

Introduction

Concerned citizens and authorities in India are now raising the potential for grey water or wastewater reuse in urban areas to deal with fresh water scarcity, especially in the dry months before the onset of the monsoon (Narain 2018; Niti Aayog 2018; Shah 2016). This interest in finding new water supplies is pushing communities, governments, and businesses to discuss, experiment with, and pilot projects to treat wastewater and recycle it. In India, many of the projects are decentralized units or small-scale treatment systems operating in a neighborhood or an institutional setting. The treated water is used on site to avoid transport of the wastewater through underground and aboveground pipes to drains or treatment plants. The planning, installation, and effective operation and maintenance of these facilities create or require changes in housing and plumbing design, institutional setup, citizen engagement, governance, and technology.

The stress on water resources in India's urban and peri-urban areas is felt by all and threatens the viability of city living on a daily basis (Sengupta 2018). Neighborhoods supplied by water tankers rather than piped water are especially stressed in terms of availability and pricing. Residents in these peri-urban or "unauthorized" locales pay more for water per kiloliter from tankers than do other citizens who pay for piped water (Anand 2017; Bjorkman 2015; Narain 2018; Niti Aayog 2018). Residents in these and other stressed zones are sometimes able to combine small amounts of water from different sources, from low-quality piped water, from RO water (reverse osmosis) supplied by private vendors and in homes, from groundwater, and water supplied by city and private tankers (Maurya et al. 2017). These pressures and recent regulatory limits and bans on groundwater use push households and businesses to find other sources and to consider treated wastewater for nonpotable purposes. This connects to trends in experimenting with decentralized or modular approaches to water and energy currently underway (Cross 2016; Gupta 2015; Sovacooll and Ramana 2015; Ulsrude et al. 2011).[2]

This paper introduces four cases of wastewater recycling that we consider functional "success" stories; these are drawn from a larger pool of 40 recycling projects that we visited and gathered data on. The argument of the paper is that a variety of successful cases are emerging and understanding the key determinants will help plot out how success can be modeled for the Indian context. We identify the key parameters that make these systems work in a flexible way. We describe the historical, institutional, regulatory, and economic pressures leading to the creation of projects and explain the key policies and regulations that impinge on this sector. The analysis will show how the parameters of leadership, water availability, water pricing, regulations, and business savings are motivating functional wastewater reuse projects. We then use these labels as heuristics for models of success in Indian conditions.

Informality, the Hydrosocial Cycle, and the Flexibat Approach

Our approach extends from previous investigations of the acceptability of water reuse schemes in India and other countries (Hurlimann and McKay 2007; Kuttuva, Lele, and Mendez 2018; Molinos-Senante, Hernández-Sancho, and Sala-Garrido 2011; Lienhoop et al. 2014 Roomratanapun 2001; Suneethi et al. 2015).[3] We also contribute to discussions on the extent to which decentralized systems can replace or complement centralized wastewater treatment systems (Arora et al. 2015). Centralized systems work best in locales where there is a fully piped sewerage network with an accoutrement of pumping stations, bioreactors and ancillary equipment such as backup generators, and materials for repairs. There is nothing close to full sewerage for cities in India and more than 70% of wastewater runs untreated to contaminate surface and ground water supplies.[4] So, the majority of studies in India cover the functioning and acceptability of small-scale decentralized units (Kuttuva, Lele, and Mendez 2018; Lienhoop et al. 2012; Ravishankar, Nautiyal, and Seshaiah 2018; Suneethi et al. 2015).[5]

Here, we approach a similar question, which is, to what extent do small-scale systems work and why? How can we find the best examples? In our research, several key concepts and approaches have been useful in orienting our perspective. First, we draw upon the understanding of informality developed by others and that we have expanded in other work (Alley 2015, 2016; Follmann 2014; Ranganathan 2016; Roy and Ong 2012; Schwartz et al. 2015). Water informality happens when the state uses laws and principles that are appropriate for the moment, but then changes those uses and even works contrary to them at a later date. Ranganathan (2016, 3) defines urban water informality as the uneven application or suspension of laws, rules, and official procedures in the governance of space and water infrastructure. The inverted notion of informality developed by Ananya Roy (2009) and reformulated by Ranganathan (2016) describes the intentional vagueness or opacity of project maps, plans, protocols, and compliance to rules and regulations. The intentional vagueness in articulating and implementing official rules and procedures helps to keep the circle of real knowledge small, so that it can be controlled by fewer people (Bear 2015, 105–122). Roy (2009, 83) has noted that the absence of land titles, the existence of fuzzy boundaries and incomplete maps, and the vagueness of policies are "the basis of state authority and serve as modes of sovereignty and discipline." We find evidence of informality in the decisions taken in infrastructure design and contracting, and in the governance and control over groundwater.

Others have toyed with ways of describing infrastructure failures in sanitation by digging deeper into the actual running of facilities and services such as in operation and maintenance. For instance, Starkl et al. (2017) have noted that hidden failures may exist behind the appearance of functioning systems and that these layers of known and hidden failures are part of the complexity of creating decentralized facilities. In terms of identifying key parameters that determine the best examples of functioning projects, we follow from Starkl et al. and their critical view of "success" and "failure" in their analysis of the functioning of decentralized wastewater facilities across India. In a recent paper focusing on 58 projects across India, they (2017, 133) qualified how they were determining success and failure as follows:

> For this paper, "apparent success" is success in the view of local experts (step 1 of data collection) and "actual success" is success in the view of a closer inspection by international expert teams (step 2). "Hidden failure" is apparent success that is not actual success. This paper emphasizes hidden failures, as the subsample of hidden failures appears to be random, justifying statistical methodology. (In step 1, data could not be collected at random, as insight by the local experts about the systems was needed. However, as hidden failures result from a lack of information, one could not intentionally search for them.) "Hidden success" was not observed.

Apart from the use in research designs and conclusions, definitions of success and failure are part of the algorithm for funding agencies at local, national, and international levels. If identified as failed systems, these projects have little hope of continued support, even in a weak administrative regime. Alternately, the aim of failure stories may be to motivate concern, attention, and investment in infrastructure. Success stories bring more funds for investment or may provide justification that no more investment is needed. In this study, we draw from our notion of infrastructure disarray (Alley et al. 2018) to assume that success and failure are not mutually exclusive categories but are determined flexibly by the operation of parameters. We see that problems in infrastructure (1) are layers of failed systems that may or may not be physically connected; and (2) can be thought of not in terms of success versus failure or presence versus nonpresence, but as a multitude of interconnected, overlapping, or disconnected segments of the sewage services chain (Alley et al. 2018).

We also draw loosely from the framework of the hydrosocial cycle as we trace out the intertwined water and society patterns that coproduce the meanings, uses, and technologies of wastewater and water consumption and production (Budds 2008; Linton 2010; Linton and Budds 2013; Swyngedouw 2009). The hydrosocial cycle accounts for the ways the society—key actors and institutions—shape water uses through and with infrastructures and technologies. The hydrosocial cycle also means the ways water flows and turns into wastewater, the ways it is transformed to another state and becomes recycled water and how all these states of water reflect, refract, and empower or disempower social relations. Included in these social meanings and uses of water are the perceptions of the microbiology of water and of the impact different kinds of water have on the body and health.

These cases indicate that the hydrosocial cycle is shifting and calibrating to new flows of water and governance over time. Water flows are being altered in three ways. One way is in water provisioning for public sector or public–private partnerships; the second way is in the governance of wastewater treatment and the operation and maintenance of facilities. The third way is in water availability wherein polluted water is converted into usable water and added to rather than thrown off from the water supply chain.

Recently, Starkl et al. (2018) have argued for a perspective called "flexibat" which denotes the best possible and workable technology for a given wastewater situation. They showed the need to understand variability in the success and failure of these sewage treatment plants (STPs). Their analysis compared costs and benefits of a number of small-scale systems, such as membrane systems, soil biotechnology, phytorid, vortex, and sequential batch reactor. It found that some technologies such as vortex are more costly than the others. Their data show that the membrane or MBR technology is best for removal of pathogens.

This paper expands the approach to flexibat by identifying the key institutional, cultural, and economic parameters that are producing the best examples of decentralized systems. This includes attention to behavior, econo-my, regulation, policy, and leadership as different but co-existing systems and structures. We will show that the key parameters of leadership, water pricing, water scarcity, regulations, and closed-loop business savings are weighted differently in each case but that all are present to some degree in each case. They are therefore significant for India and stand to become best scenarios over time.

Wastewater providers and recyclers are not like water mafias (Ranganathan 2014) and valve or key men (Anand 2017; Dasgupta 2015) who hold power as water brokers, tanker owners, and operators. Rather they operate as "experiments" and "pilots" and often struggle with financing and repairs. There has been a general disinterest among government and citizen groups to engage in improvements with wastewater treatment; therefore, the projects we highlight are a welcome advancement.

Methodology and Verification

For this paper, we chose four cases that best represent the range of activities taking place across 40 sites we visited over a three-year period. To choose these cases, we surveyed 40 projects that we located through the advice of key NGO members, industry actors and companies, and the information provided in the databases of the Centre for Science and Environment, the Central Pollution Control Board (CPCB), the National Mission Clean Ganga (NMCG), and other engaged agencies. Snowball sampling techniques were also used to identify the persons with knowledge of projects at each facility location. Several research groups led by Indian Institute of Technology (IIT) professors were especially helpful in sharing information on existing STPs and their creators and funders and introducing the projects with the most effective performances. These teams of researchers also helped us gain access to functioning projects, given that it is up to the project owners or facility owners to decide whether they will allow a researcher entry and grant permission to collect water samples and interview project members.

Among the 40 sites we visited, we found a range of recycling projects at industries, university campuses, hospital grounds, housing complexes, neighborhoods, airports, malls, and city parks. In these, we identified five key parameters that we found across all sites to varying degrees (Frijns et al. 2016). We identified these key parameters after analysis of data collected at each site using qualitative focus groups, structured interviews, and participant observation. Key informants, official and company records, NGO reports, and university research projects were used as sampling frames for the conduct of focus groups and interviews at many of the sites we visited. Interviews with officials in the Ministries of Environment, Forests and Climate Change, Water Resources; Power; Renewables, Central and State Pollution Control Boards, the Sanitation departments of municipalities and other councils such as the NDMC produced an understanding of government interest and acceptability as well as in-

stitutional regulations and procedures. In interviews with authorities, project monitors, NGOs, and university teams, we explored institutional constraints and possibilities and technological innovations and limitations. Generally, in each site, we conducted 3–5 focus groups and 20–30 structured interviews to find convergence regarding important themes. Research reports, maps, feasibility reports, detailed project reports, and ecology, wildlife, and landscape projects were also collected and analyzed.

Selection of Cases and Key Parameters

In this paper, we introduce four cases of water reuse to show four functioning systems representing government, public–private partnerships, and business arrangements, and we discuss the working of key parameters for each case. We are concerned with overall functionality and with significant parameters that we have identified through the survey of 40 projects. Our survey led us to identify (1) leadership, (2) water pricing, (3) water availability, (4) regulations, and (5) business savings as the key parameters in the functioning of these projects. Departing from other studies that we reference later, we did not include the broad label of "acceptability" as a parameter. Since some of the projects we have investigated do not have a user public associated with them, acceptability of public or private users was considered more specifically in terms of leadership and the decisions that are made in the face of scarcity, pricing, and regulations and court orders.

We focused on the human determinants of functionality and did not assess technological adequacy, efficiency, or success.[6] We draw upon other recent reports for those measures (see Starkl et al. 2018). We are concretizing the notion of success here to mean a project that can reduce contamination of the ecological or hydrological system to a degree deemed to be an improvement from an immediately previous condition. The understandings of previous conditions and improvements are taken from information provided in the focus groups and interviews with concerned authorities, scientists, and citizens.

The four cases involve large agencies and/or businesses: the NDMC, a government agency; IIT-M, an autonomous government institution; the Keshopur Bus Depot, a public–private partnership; and the Marriott hotel, a fully private enterprise. The similarity among these cases is that all the water-consuming entities have to buy water from the government institutions responsible for water supply. These government institutions are the Delhi Jal Board (or DJB) in the case of the garden STPs and the Keshopur Bus Depot; the Chennai Metro Water Supply Board in the case of IIT-M; and the Brihannmumbai Water Supply Board in the case of the Marriott Hotel. The two main push factors in these cases are: (1) National Green Tribunal (hereafter NGT) orders on mandatory treatment and reuse of wastewater and (2) the NGT and Central Groundwater Commission limits or bans on the use of groundwater.[7] Apart from explaining these external push determinants, we also describe how variously positioned agents (as managers, scientists, and company members) discuss these treatment infrastructures, the microbial reactions that produce this water and the trace metals, substances, and pathogens remaining in the treated water. In these discussions, water values are directly related to the mechanics of technologies. Producers and consumers see the waters produced at different stages of treatment and recycling as differentiated forms. As Barnes (2014) has argued for irrigation water reuse in Egypt and Bjorkman (2015) has for Mumbai supply, water is not simply water, but becomes different waters, in terms of quality and quantity over time and space.[8]

The Bus Depot: Situated Categories of Water

Water recycling is now a legal requirement for large institutional users of water such as industries, universities, housing complexes, and five-star hotels.[9] With these requirements come readjustments in the ways citizens define their water sources and the relative quality they impute to each source. In general, most of our interviews with project communities revealed that recycled wastewater is considered inappropriate for direct human uses, but companies and municipalities are realizing its potential to supply nonessential or nonhuman contact uses, such as water for horticulture, toilet flushing, and industrial processes. This means that users are categorizing water supplies in new ways and directing that specific uses be made for each supply category. This demonstrates trends in water classification that are based on location-specific supplies and their qualities, and these classifications may vary depending on context.[10]

In west Delhi, as 125 buses enter the depot, about 45 buses are washed every day. The employees of this depot are reliant on recycled wastewater to do this cleaning. In the bus depot, employees use four categories to define their sources. These are: (1) potable water treated from surface water sources and provided by the DJB, (2) groundwater that is not treated, (3) treated wastewater that is piped from a decentralized project across the street, and (4) tanker water carrying poorly treated wastewater from a conventional, centralized STP across the street. Potable water is the purest for human consumption with degrading qualities in the other categories. When talking in Hindi, these employees used the English word "pure" to describe water from the DJB. Groundwater is preferable to treated wastewater. In some cases, however, employees remarked that in emergency situations, they have had to drink this recycled water.

Before 2016, there was only one company that had produced a viable decentralized pilot plant in Delhi (STPs). This was Absolute Water, a company spin-off from a large industrial sugar company. The owner realized that industries could recycle their water for reuse and see significant savings and a more reliable water supply. After installing a plant in their own industry, they convinced the DJB to let them build a pilot project on the campus of the Kes-hopur Sewage treatment facility in west Delhi. The DJB had enough land there to house the project. The company used its own funds to construct the plant on the vermiculture model that uses biomass and earthworms to bring down the biological content of the wastewater. The water is then passed through a carbon filter and a membrane to produce near bacteria-free water that can be considered potable quality water according to WHO standards. The facility is powered by a solar panel and uses 8 kW of energy to produce 100 kiloliters of water each day. The Delhi Chief Minister Kejriwal inaugurated the pilot plant on July 9, 2015, with a media blitz in which he was photographed drinking the treated water. Absolute Water operated the plant for a year before the DJB agreed to assume the operation and maintenance. Then the DJB found a user for this product in the bus depot across the street and laid a pipeline to bring the treated water to them.

The definitions and categories of water were immediately apparent in our discussions with the employees of the bus depot. Those working in the bus depot have a working knowledge of each source and a strong awareness of the differences between the four kinds of water they use. They are, in terms of their own labels: DJB piped water which comes from the water treatment plant at Wazirabad and is used for drinking; treated wastewater from the Keshopur pilot plant, called "pipeline STP water" or "Kejriwal pani"; treated wastewater coming from the Keshopur STP called "tanker water" and groundwater. In order of quality, the DJB piped (drinking) water is the best, but there was a close second with Kejriwal water. The poorest quality was the water coming from the large conventional STP that they call tanker water.

In other words, there are two pipelines supplying water to the depot. One brings drinking water from the DJB's water treatment plant and the other brings treated wastewater from the pilot project that uses earthworms and filters. The pipeline water from the pilot project is the most important, as it is the water used to wash the buses in the depot. On the day of our interview, there was a discussion about quality, with some explaining that clearer is better and that it must be without smell and bad taste to be useful beyond horticulture. In the following discussion, NM and AK are the researchers and the others are employees at the bus depot.[11]

UK: This is the govt. order based on court order ... and of NGT too ... they forbid us so we stopped this bore well, as in our department we need to issue foreclosure, we did the same and sent the report. Then we had this STP pipeline and then this water supply started. You know, previously we were fully dependent upon tanker-waters. In two days, we had to use three tankers.

NM: 30,000 l water.

UK: Yes, as we have 125 buses ... so around 45 buses get washed daily ... we do deep cleaning means cleaning from inside and washing from outside too. So we cannot wash all the buses in one day ...

AK: So he said that he saved groundwater? Now no more use of groundwater?

NM: No ... So you don't use groundwater at all?

UK: I will show you ... we have stopped our submersible ... because there is the strict order about this.

NM: So, now you water your gardens with STP water only?

UK: Yes.

NM: And you wash your buses with this water only?

UK: We wash our vehicles 100% with this water only.

NM: So, if someday there is no piped water then what do you do for gardening?

UK: In that case, we use remaining tanker water. After washing the vehicles if water remains in the tanker we use it for gardening ... you know tanker water is not as clean as the STP pipeline water ... I will show you the waters.

NM: From where do you get this tanker water.

UK: That water also comes from DJB Keshopur but from a different plant. It is not filtered water. So, what have you seen in the plant, tanker water does not get filtered.

AK: So ... that water comes from the big plant, not through the membrane filter ...

Em: It has some smell too ...

UK: They collect water in a tank and filter it and give it to us in a tanker, whereas the piped water they again pass it through the filter and then pump it to us.

NM: So STP pipe water is coming through the Kejriwal Point, and water by tanker is not from the Kejriwal point?

UK: Yes ... both are different.

NM: They are saying there is smell in the tanker water.

AK: Of course, we have just seen the outflow from the STP in the big drain ... it's too smelly and water is very dirty ...

UK: They make fertilizers from that ...

NM: They call it sludge ...

UK: You have had seen that on the back side they have a tank where they collect treated water. In that tank, there are wood saw and earthworms, these earthworm feed on that dirty water and clean it, purify it, then what comes out is this water ... they replace it about in six months ... they pour new earthworms ... to clean the water ... earthworms survive on dirt ...

AK: So, he is talking about the same treatment plant of Kejriwal ... have seen that ... and that water comes here.

UK: Tanker water is not from this plant, it is from the STP only ...

NM: It means tanker is not taking water from Kejriwal point but taking water

before this point.

AK: Because Kejriwal points water comes here for vehicles ... this is the best water from that treatment plant, by using earthworms etc.

....

Em: What difference we will have in groundwater and DJB water, the same difference is here too ... groundwater would look clean and clear in a glass and DJB water would also look the same but only a machine can tell you about the quality of water.

AK: So, the water which comes from Kejeriwal's plant that does not have smell ...

UK: No..

Em: They add some chemical in it ... separately.

UK: They filter it and then add ...

AK: Add chlorine ...

UK: No, not chlorine, they add something else ...

Em: They add some chemical.

AK: Okay, so a membrane is there and water goes through the membrane and becomes drinkable.

UK: Yes ... They have written there very clearly and I have seen that ... and perhaps they have shown Kejriwal drinking this water...

NM: Yes.

UK: So when their Engineer came, who

has laid this pipeline. He said that not drinkable but not less than drinking quality. Means, there is still some inadequacy in this.

NM: But this is a good phrase—not drinkable but not less than drinking quality.

AK: Not worth to drink but not less than the quality of drinking water ... not drinkable means, there is no acceptance in the heart ...

UK: There still some minor particles ...

NM: So you believe that there is some ...

UK: Means, my heart says there is some defect in this water ...

Em: Madam, if one will not get water then one may drink this also ...

This discussion clearly shows that the bus depot employees have a detailed knowledge of categories of water that are provided to them and that the researchers are co-producing this knowledge through their questions as well. The employees conduct a personal evaluation of each based on daily contact and some usage. Their knowledge is an interactive and cumulative knowledge generated from experience and some understanding of the biological and microbial processes by which the wastewater is treated. They are co-producing their knowledge in some measure of interaction with the wastewater engineers and water scientists active across the street in the government sewage treatment facility. This detailed conversation helps to show that apart from the critical need to find sources

of water to clean the buses, experiential learning is most important in generating acceptability of using this treated water. In addition, users are able to distinguish the qualities of various water supplies provided to them based on experiential practices such as sniffing and tasting. This is the practical knowledge that produces the choice for sustained usage. While a survey of literature by Fielding, Dolnicar, and Schultz (2018) found that acceptance of recycled water drops with increasing human contact, this case shows that the consumers' experience of using the treated water for a specific purpose (cleaning buses) and seeing and smelling its quality are strong motivators for the functionality or the "success" of the project.[12]

This depot is a public–private partnership between Delhi Transport Corporation and TATA Motors. The public sector entity and the private company that together run the depot pay three different rates for these three categories of water. They pay Rs. 7 per kiloliter for the STP pipeline water and Rs. 140 per kiloliter for the STP tanker water, which are both used for washing. Before the STP pipeline water supply started, they were drawing up groundwater with an electric pump. The estimated cost of the electrical pumping roughly prices groundwater at around Rs. 10 per kiloliter. In theory, there is savings to the partnership by shifting from groundwater to the new pipeline water from the pilot STP.[13]

This case mentions the motivating roles of the Central Groundwater Authority (CGWA) and NGT in ordering large water users to discontinue use of groundwater. Generally, regulatory power resides with these ministries and departments: the CGWA, the Ministry of Environment, Forests and Climate Change, the CPCB, the state Pollution Control Boards, the High Courts and Supreme Court, and now the NGT. Regulation occurs as a series of actions that impose rules, limits, and punishments on individuals, companies, and government offices. Citizens can also lead these efforts or contest them through petitions and participation in the NGT. However, it is important to understand where real regulatory power or pressure resides and this depends upon the state or region of the country. In the northern Indian states of Uttarakhand, Himachal Pradesh, Uttar Pradesh, and Bihar, the CGWA and the NGT rather than the MoEFCC, or the PCBs in the sanitation field exert more power. In Tamil Nadu and Karnataka, the State Pollution Control Boards exert more influence.[14] Across India, the policy shells of Namami Gange and Swachha Bharat help to set criteria or benchmarks for projects and provide the vision and mission for sanitation but play no role in regulation.[15] The Namami Ganga and Swachha Bharat programs also provide leadership in terms of policy vision and rhetoric. In terms of infrastructure, the Smart Cities program is providing a set of criteria for urban improvement which includes physical infrastructure and social infrastructure. On the physical infrastructure side, the government is promoting smart grid, smart roads, parking, solar power, water ATMs, and STPs (Bahinipati 2017).

A short history of groundwater regulations helps to explain how it emerged in importance as a driver for water recycling. In 2013, the NGT began a series of debates on groundwater usage and contamination in the context of petitions filed by citizens on water and sewage problems. In eight different cases, the NGT ruled that industries or other large quantity users must curb their use of groundwater (Charts 1–3). They ordered that large quantity groundwater users must obtain an NOC, or no objection permit, from the CGWA.[16] In addition, households were forbidden from using bore well water for gardening and horticulture, but this rule has been hard to enforce and monitor. Over time, new permits have become harder to procure. In the new draft guidelines of the Groundwater Bill in Parliament, this renewal period varies: for individuals, it is set at every five years, for industries, at every three years, and for real estate projects, at every two years. The draft guidelines also take out the need to recharge groundwater.[17] The bill advocates strengthening the regulatory powers of gram sabhas, panchayats, and municipal bodies related to groundwater. However, some argue these new guidelines are "trying to make a system wherein state or district level authorities will be giving NOCs but whether those authorities have capacity to give NOCs after understanding the implications is the question" (Sandrp 2017). It is within this context of regulating groundwater extraction that a stronger direction to use recycled wastewater has emerged.

Chart 1. Proposed Bills

1.	Model Bill for the Conservation, Protection, Regulation and Management of Groundwater, 2016	Gives emphasis on rainwater harvesting and recycling and reuse of water "for non-potable urban, industrial, and agricultural use, as well as augmentation of potable water supplies through indirect reuse." Without a permit issued by the appropriate authority no groundwater abstraction is permitted for nonpotable use, and for industrial and infrastructure projects
2	Draft National Water Framework Bill, 2016	States that (1) The appropriate Government shall make all efforts for appropriate treatment of wastewater and its gainful utilization (2) The appropriate Government shall evolve and implement economic models that promote sustainability of recycle-reduce-and-reuse of water resources, while ensuring adherence to principles of equity
3	Draft Model Building Bye-laws, 2015	Mandates rain water harvesting structures in all buildings having a plot size of 100 sq. m or more. And "All building having a minimum discharge of 10,000 litre. and above per day shall incorporate waste water recycling system. The recycled water should be used for horticultural purposes."

1. http://mowr.gov.in/sites/default/files/Model_Bill_Groundwater_May_2016_0.pdf

2. http://mowr.gov.in/sites/default/files/Water_Framework_18July_2016%281%29.pdf

3. http://mohua.gov.in/upload/uploadfiles/files/Draft%20MBBL-2015.pdf

Chart 2. Key Legal Framework and Accountable Institutions

1.	The Water (Prevention and Control of Pollution) Act, 1974 — Implementation of the Water (Prevention and Control of Pollution) Act, 1974 which seeks to restore water quality —Monitoring of treated sewage and trade effluents and to use recycled water in agriculture	CPCB/SPCB and PCC

2.	The Water (Prevention and Control of Pollution) Cess Act, 1977 — All Industries and Local Authority have to pay water cess. Provision of rebate in the case of installation of STP or ETP, as the case may be	CPCB/SPCB/ ULB/ Local Authority
3.	Environment (Protection) Act, 1986 under section 3(3) —constitution of CGWA "to regulate and control, management and development of ground water in the country and to issue necessary regulatory direction for the purpose"	CGWA

Chart 3. Key Cases

Sl. no.	Cases	Order
1.	M.C. Mehta versus Union of India and Anr., 1997(11), SSC312 Order date: December 10, 1996	The Supreme Court advised to constitute a CGWB, "As an Authority" for regulating the "indiscriminate boring and withdrawal of underground water in the country"
2.	Vikrant Kumar Tongad V/s Union of India & Ors. Order date: January 11, 2013	NGT directed "All the places in the Noida and Greater Noida not to extract any quantity of ground water for the purpose of construction or otherwise"
3.	Krishan Kant Singh versus M/s Deoria Paper Ltd. Order date: April 15, 2015	NGT directed to Central Ground Water Authority that "it shall be obligatory upon it to ensure that any person operating tubewell or any means to extract groundwater should obtain its permission and should operate the same subject to law in force, even if such unit is existing unit or the unit is still to be established"

4.	Yogesh Nagar versus Union of India & Ors. Order Date: December 10, 2015	In an important case related to the industries in the state of Uttar Pradesh, The NGT ordered that "All industries falling in any category and which are extracting Ground water would be required to obtain permission from the CGWA positively by 31st December, 2015. If they fail to obtain such permission and comply with the directions of the Board, the CGWA and the UPPCB shall take action in accordance with law"
5.	Mukesh Yadav versus State of Uttar Pradesh and Others. Order date: February 29, 2016	NGT ordered that "Greater NOIDA Authority shall in consultation with the CGWA issue guideline for ensuring that the future constructions permitted in the area take into account the status of ground water table and impose appropriate restrictions on digging below the ground water level for the purposes of construction of basements in the multi-story buildings/apartments and other related activities." For construction activity water should be drawn from STPs
6.	Paryavaran Suraksha Samiti and another versus Union of India & Ors. (writ Petition (C) No. 375 of 2012) Order date: February 22, 2017	The Supreme Court made it mandatory for the industries to have a functional primary effluent treatment plants and need to install a functional common effluent treatment plants within the given time for continuation of industrial activity and also to have an online effluent/emission monitoring system
7.	Sushil Raghav & Anr. versus Central Ground Water Authority & Ors. Order date: April 13, 2017	NGT ordered CGWA to ensure that no private individual, person or builder is allowed to extract ground water without permission or a valid NOC
8.	Shailesh Singh versus Hotel Jaypee Vasant, New Delhi and Others (M.A. No. 1333 of 2015) Order date: August 14, 2018	NGT ordered concerned hotels to seek permission and inform CGWA the time period for their extraction of ground water and monthly quantity extracted. NGT ordered CGWA to take action if the extraction was "in excess of the permissible limit".

1. http://cgwb.gov.in/cgwa/NGT/NGT%20Order%20on%20Industries%20in%20BISRAKH.pdf

2. http://cgwb.gov.in/cgwa/NGT/NGT%20order%20dated%2015th%20April%202015.pdf

3. http://cgwb.gov.in/cgwa/Documents/NGT%20ORDER%20DT.%2013.4.17%20SUSHIL%20RAGHAV%20VS%20CGWA.pdf

4. http://cgwb.gov.in/cgwa/NGT/Judgement%20order%20in%20MA%20No%2021%20of%202015%20in%20Application%20No%2047%20of%202015.pdf

5. http://cgwb.gov.in/cgwa/NGT/NGT%20order%20dated%2030.11.2015.pdf

6. http://cgwb.gov.in/cgwa/NGT/OA%20133%20OF%2014%20JUDGMENT%20%20IN%20MUKESH%20YADAV.pdf

7. http://www.uppcb.com/pdf/writ-prtition_080317.pdf

8. http://www.greentribunal.gov.in/DisplayFile.aspx

Garden STPs under the NDMC

Now, we turn to the other projects in the Delhi region. There is a new push to set up decentralized STPs in the National Capital Region to provide this treated wastewater to the city gardens. A group of political and administrative leaders within the Delhi legislature and the New Delhi Municipal Council is driving this initiative. The Chief Minister of Delhi and the Chairman of the NDMC are the most visible leaders. Electricity, water, and sanitation were key issues in the party's campaign, and the party through the NDMC has initiated a number of sanitation, water, and electricity projects since 2015.

In September 2017, the Chief Minister Kejriwal took over the water portfolio in the Delhi government to assume a more hands on approach to reforms in the water sector. Earlier in his position as Chief Minister, Kejriwal had initiated water reforms by reducing the tariff for household water services (Pandey 2015). The tariff structure in 2015 included up to 20 kiloliters of free water with nominal charges for households. The CM called this lifeline water that should be provided to all residents. After a short time, however, the DJB and others protested that the city could not afford such a gracious provision and the volumetric rate was set at a low rate to recover at least some revenue for households using less than 20 kiloliter a month.

The New Delhi Municipal Council region consumes around 125 million liters per day (mld) of potable water,

120 mld of which it buys from the DJB for around Rs. 15 a kiloliter. Bore wells and rainwater harvesting make up the rest of the need. The estimated cost to procure groundwater is around Rs. 10 a kiloliter. The NDMC then distributes the 125 mld of water purchased from the DJB through its pipe grids and by water tankers to nonpiped areas. It is sold according to a revised rate scheme that gives the first 20 kiloliters of water at the rate of 3.45 per kiloliters with scaled rates above that.[18] These household uses are therefore heavily subsidized and the NDMC must earn higher rates from big users if it wants to recoup its costs. About 10% of the NDMC's water budget is used for maintenance of the city gardens and for other beautification structures such as fountains and lakes. This also has no user fees associated with it, so the cost is covered by the NDMC directly.

In the area controlled by the New Delhi Municipal Council, or Lutyen's Delhi, a number of beautiful gardens create an aesthetic ambiance for the capital. The New Delhi Municipal Council uses about 80 mld of water to maintain around 8,000 parks; until recently, this need has been supplied by a small amount of NDMC "pure" water and the rest from groundwater and treated wastewater from the Okhla STP. The DJB estimates that the total water treated at its STPs is about 455 million gallons a day (mgd) of which they claim to provide 142 mgd (or 645 mld) of treated water for horticulture and irrigation across the Delhi metropolitan region.[19] While it is difficult to verify whether this treated water is actually

107

being used in the areas surrounding the city's STPs, it is more realistic to suppose that the treated wastewater from the closest STP in Okhla has been partially used for the NDMC parks. Several individuals in the CPWD described a "filtered water" pipeline from the Okhla STP to the NDMC garden areas. With groundwater levels depleting to over 300 feet in some sections of Delhi, there has been increasing focus on curtailing use of groundwater for horticulture and other nonessential services. In this context, in 2017, the NGT directed all urban municipalities to use treated wastewater for horticulture.

Figure 1. Map of decentralized STPs in the National Capital Region (created by Pratibha Prakash)

In March 2016, the New Delhi Municipal Council took the decision to promote decentralized STPs to help deal with the wastewater load in the city and promote recycling of treated water for functions such as horticulture and irrigation. The amount of usable water produced by these decentralized plants would then greatly supplement the minor supply they were receiving from the Okhla STP. The NDMC installed eight decentralized STPs and has plans to create over 10 more within its jurisdiction. These projects will help to reduce the dependency on groundwater and begin a separation of fresh and contaminated water. Fresh water sources from the upper catchments of the Ganga and

Yamuna rivers could be better protected from pollution if wastewater were diverted away from in stream flows and used in this manner after treatment.

At present, there are two private companies working with the NDMC to construct and maintain these new STPs. Ecosystem Resource Management Pvt Ltd has built five plants (four operating and one under construction) on the Soil Biotechnology model invented by Professor Shankar's team at IIT-Bombay. Over the last 20 years, M.Sc. and Ph.D. students have developed and tested the soil biotechnology approach and it is now a patented method for wastewater treatment. The plants are built quickly and operated with low skilled labor. They require very little power and take up much less land than conventional plants, for instance, 500 m² for a 500 kld plant. The other company working with the NDMC is SS Engineering Corporation. They have built two plants on the MBR or Membrane Bioreactor model and a third is under construction. This method requires very little land but consumes more electrical power in the activated sludge process. Sludge is generated every day, so it must be collected and distributed for horticulture and irrigation. The plants range in treatment capacity from 100 to 500 kiloliters per day. The NDMC plans to install other smaller units like these in schools and housing colonies. These smaller projects will be undertaken by NEERI—the National Environmental Engineering Research Institute—using their own patented phytorid technology. All of the STPs in this NDMC cluster draw their wastewater from a nearby drain or

nala, and avoid the need to build long pipelines from point sources of wastewater. The longest pipeline is around 750 m. The specific arrangement in the public–private partnership between the NDMC and the company is that the company covers most of the costs involved in building and maintaining the sanitation supply chain. These costs include laying pipelines from the nearest wastewater source to the plant, treatment plant building costs, and operation and maintenance costs for 12 years. The installation costs include procuring, financing, plant construction, staff for operation and maintenance, water storage, and distribution. Over the whole system, a significant savings occurs by removing the need to transport the wastewater long distances to a treatment plant. It is simply a matter of tapping in to the subterranean tunnels of wastewater coursing underneath every part of the city. But land is a significant challenge and the NDMC case is unique in that available space in the parks can be utilized for these projects without causing any displacement. The tighter land situation in other cities may restrict the feasibility of decentralized STPs. STPs in the NDMC area are located in the parks maintained by the NDMC, so the scope for community participation is minimal.

In these garden projects, the contract between the government and the company defines the capital and maintenance responsibilities of both parties. In that contract, the NDMC agrees to buy all the water produced by the plant while allowing access to the city wastewater drain where the raw supply is drawn. The NDMC also provides the land for the STP at no cost to the private operator and then distributes the treated water, at its own cost, through water tankers to other gardens in the territory. The NDMC pays a rate between 30 and 37 Rs. per kiloliter to the company for the days that they collect the treated water and then adds a lower rated payment for those days that they cannot collect the water due to weather or other circumstances. The private company in theory should be able to pay off its investment and glean a profit from these regular payments made by the NDMC after about five or six years. The NDMC on the other hand does not have to come up with the initial capital for the project but pays over time by guaranteeing to purchase the water. This decentralizes water governance to the location of the facility but maintains institutional controls through government pricing and a guarantee to purchase the treated water. In this case, the government entity becomes the consumer rather than the producer, thus altering the hydrosocial cycle.

Figure 2. Rose garden with an SBT plant in the foreground, located along Shantipath near Embassies and Consulates. (Picture by Kelly D. Alley)

Closed-Loop or "Zero Discharge" Cases

In Karnataka and Tamil Nadu, the Pollution Control Boards are now requiring industries, housing societies, and five-star hotels to use recycled wastewater for gardening, toilet flushing, and industrial processes.[20] There are only a few water recycling projects in the country that can be considered closed-loop or zero discharge. They are interesting models and propose the most dramatic shifts in the hydrosocial cycle. They transform consumers into producer–consumers and this has interesting implications for governance over wastewater management.

The two projects we introduce as case studies are located in large institutional–business complexes. One is at the IIT in Chennai and the other is in the Renaissance Hotel and Convention Center in Mumbai. Both their systems were developed to help solve water-scarcity problems. The IIT needed water for its sprawling campus at a time when city provisions were running very short. Engineering professors were instrumental in getting the university administration to invest in a state-of-the-art system to recycle wastewater and re-engineer the entire campus for dual plumbing.[21] With a population of about 20,000, of which 9,000 are students, 9,000 are residents, and 2,000 constitute a floating population, the institute's one-day requirement is 2.8 mld and the Chennai Metro Water and Sewage Board supplies 1.2–1.8 mld of pure water. The gap is bridged by treated wastewater on site. Their STP provides recycled water for toilet flushing in the dormitories, for campus gardening, air conditioning, and other building and cleaning needs. The facility was built in a phased manner, at a cost of about 20 crores (Krishna Chaitanya and Krishna 2017). During the drought of 2015, the campus was able to function with very little city water, using their own internal resources through recycling. The lead professor in this effort recently explained to the Indian Express:

> The IIT-M STP treats close to 30 lakh [3 million litres per day], including 8 lakh litres [800,000 litres per day] of wastewater generated by the IIT-M research park. They send back 8 lakh litres of treated water to the research park for their utilization and 10 lakh litres is routed for flushing and upkeep of greenery. So the remaining 10–12 lakh litres is in excess, which is being diverted into ponds. Once those are full, two groundwater recharge wells are dug up, each having a capacity of 0.5 MLD. This will replenish the fresh water lake. Overall, nothing is wasted. (Krishna Chaitanya and Krishna 2017)

The second closed-loop system is in the Renaissance Hotel and Conference Center in Mumbai. The Manager of the Engineering department explains that they were first motivated to upgrade and fully utilize their own STP after water shortage affected their ability to run the AC cooling towers for three very large high-rise hotel buildings. At that time, they had a smaller

STP and were using the treated water for horticulture. They decided to upgrade the facility by creating two STPs with capacities to treat 750 and 650 kld underground at the back side of the complex. This provided more than enough water for their AC cooling towers, for flushing toilets, and for watering the gardens. The Management was able to install dual or double plumbing in the entire hotel to enable them to use recycled water for flushing toilets and city piped (pure) water for the kitchen, faucets, and showers in the rooms. The problem with older hotels, the Manager explained, is that they do not have the separate plumbing. It is hard to re-plumb and lay pipelines where they would have to shut down part of the hotel and lose revenue or disturb the guests. The manager explained:

> The challenge is that the old hotels do not have the separate piping system for flushing. Most have one pipe system for all uses in bathroom. The properties that have separate line for flushing can easily do it. A few old hotels have it but not all. Retro fit is expensive and its hard to do in a hotel where we cannot disturb guests and can't shut down because we will loose revenue. But now all new hotels and malls are designing for separate lines. Before water was readily available in India but now it is not available. It is not the case now that we have all the water we need. The water table is going down to 250 ft or more. It is too

much. It used to be 20–30 ft. So that is why everyone is thinking about how to save the water. So they are thinking of recycling but we need to reduce our use also. So we are going for low flow aerators for wash basin. 4.5 liter/minute plus dual flushing system. We have completed one building for low flow in the wash basin. It is 10.8 liter per minute in the other buildings.[22]

They see direct savings in water bills (Chart 4). He continued:

> The regulation is one thing. It is our responsibility to give back to society. We can afford to have more fresh water but if we do that means someone is getting less. It is affecting our overall bottom line. In 2015, we were having problem from [our] STP and were not getting enough water. We went for upgradation. That time using for gardening and a little bit for cooling tower. We were using a little for flushing but mixing it with fresh water in the tank before going to the rooms. Then we did modification and we have reduced intake consumption by 45%. We get 110 Rs per kiloliter. That is our cost. So if I am getting 400 kiloliter from STP everyday I am saving. Plus you get a good feeling that you are doing your bit. It doesn't go under CSR because it is a requirement.

Chart 4. Matrix of Key Parameters for the Case Studies
(Strong, Medium, and Weak)

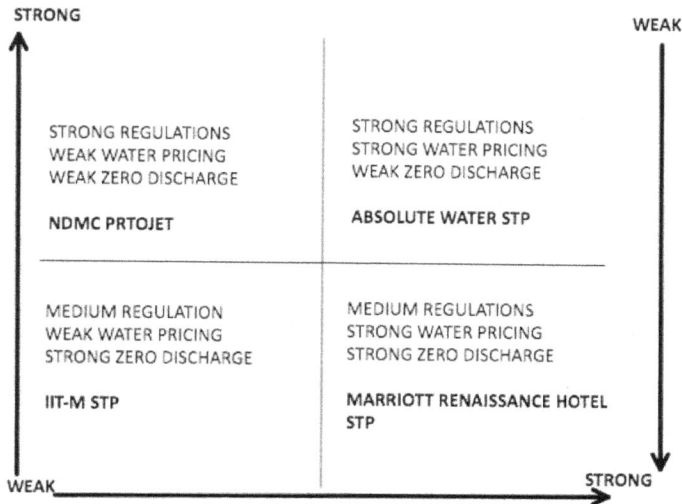

STRONG   WEAK

STRONG REGULATIONS WEAK WATER PRICING WEAK ZERO DISCHARGE **NDMC PRTOJET**	STRONG REGULATIONS STRONG WATER PRICING WEAK ZERO DISCHARGE **ABSOLUTE WATER STP**
MEDIUM REGULATION WEAK WATER PRICING STRONG ZERO DISCHARGE **IIT-M STP**	MEDIUM REGULATIONS STRONG WATER PRICING STRONG ZERO DISCHARGE **MARRIOTT RENAISSANCE HOTEL STP**

WEAK   STRONG

Emerging Scenarios

The key parameters in these case studies can be profiled into scenario types or heuristics to provide guidance on what works, taking a flexible approach (see Chart 1). The scenario types are: "interested leader," "water availability squeeze," "water pricing," "rule bearing push," and "closed loop business savings." These labels help to identify current determinants of successes and should point attention to areas of importance to be strengthened in other projects around the country.

Interested Leader

Each of the four cases has the involvement of strong leadership, where the interest of the leader is in water conservation, increasing their water supply, reducing the use of groundwater, and saving money on the water bill. In the garden STPs in Delhi and at the bus depot, leadership provided by the Delhi Government and especially key figures such as Chief Minister Kejriwal strengthens the projects in terms of investment, joint public–private responsibility, and sustainability over time. In the IIT-M case, an engineering professor was instrumental in getting the campus STP established, funded, and equipped with monitoring tools for ongoing research purposes. In the Marriott case, the engineering manager led the efforts to upgrade and expand their onsite STP and this led to big savings in their water bill and a state-of-the-art dual plumbing system throughout the hotel. These cases show that leadership is diverse but critical to a project's success. Other kinds of leadership may emerge in other projects and this heuristic should direct inquiry toward those motivators in the hope that they will be supported.

Water Pricing

These decentralized STPs are systems that will have problems and we have seen many with one problem or another. However, it is a success in sewage management if local or on-site projects are able to deliver treated water for reuse within the same cost structure provided to citizens to purchase pure water. Water tariffs (for pure water) are either fixed or too low and it is difficult for service providers to recover costs from user charges and promote water conservation (Raghavendra 2006). Since surface water provided by a city or municipal department is subsidized and scaled, we expect that treated wastewater would need to be priced and scaled accordingly to attract the interest of consumers. Pricing may motivate industry and business users more convincingly than it motivates middle class, piped water users since the rates are so much higher for them and piped water is underpriced and subsidized for the low consuming general public. A rebate in prices after installation of recycling facilities may motivate users in housing complexes, but more research is needed on that. The unpiped consumers living in unpiped, peri-urban, or unauthorized zones may be more motivated to use treated wastewater since their water tanker prices are so high.[23]

Rule-Bearing Push

A significant amount of effort has been spent in motivating the government to do an effective job of wastewater management, and many of the discussions in the NGT reflect the fact that these tasks are not done well if at all (Alley 2002, 2014, 2015; Rohilla and Dwivedi 2013; Sanghi 2014; Tare and Roy 2015). Several state and central government agencies have imposed restrictions on using potable water for nonpotable purposes and have restricted groundwater use for horticulture and gardening and some industrial processes. The NGT stands out as the primary pusher of ground breaking rules that require new behaviors such as the limits and bans on groundwater use. The named implementing agencies, the Central Groundwater Commission and the Pollution Control Boards, must enforce these orders. We can expect more push from the NGT over time and conclude that a strong, legal apparatus is a critical motivator of improvements in sanitation and water supply and delivery.

Water Availability Crunch

All the projects we have surveyed including the four featured in this paper require new kinds of relationships between government, private, and public sector entities. Although private sector involvement is considered risky, these projects show specific kinds of public–private partnerships and their conditions. This helps to understand what works in terms of contracts and responsibilities over time. In terms of adding more expertise to this sector, projects may extend the reach of reforms since most government bodies cannot take up all the needed initiatives on their own. A broad-scale addition of public–private projects could make a significant change in the hydrosocial cycle by putting more usable water into the supply chain and reducing the amount of untreated wastewater that contaminates the good water of rivers and lakes. The garden projects put treated wastewater back into the soil where the soil biology and oxygen treat the wastewater even further. The projects also reduce the need to make large extractions of groundwater for horticulture. If done on a larger scale, these substitutions could have a noticeable effect on groundwater tables.

Closed-Loop Business Savings

Two of the cases show that entities requiring a large quantity of water on a daily basis are more motivated to create their own closed-loop systems and become producers as well as consumers over time. These wastewater reuse projects create closed-loop systems in the urban hydrosocial cycle. The IIT-M project and the Renaissance hotel project circulate water along a tighter path through treatment to business/institution use and then back into treatment.

In these two closed-loop projects, there is a devolution of responsibility for operating and maintaining the facility to the local level. There is also a devolution of control over water use through the reuse of existing supply. The local level means at the functioning of the STP or within the business, university, or housing society. In a business such as the Renaissance hotel, the hotel management is responsible for operation and maintenance of the STP, not the state-level engineering or water agency as is the case with centralized STPs (Alley 2002, 2014; Sanghi 2014).

Likewise at IIT-M, engineering professors and their students are involved in monitoring the facilities as they are operated by university staff. This alters the roles of consumers and transforms them into operators and monitors. They are generating their own resource and then handling its reuse within their own community. It is a closed loop of responsibility, even though the requirement to recycle comes from the state and central pollution control boards, the municipalities, and the NGT.

This paper has argued that wastewater recycling is on the rise and can lead to significant contributions to water supply while reducing the pollution load on precious surface waters. These cases point attention to key parameters of success that can be identified and supported in other cases around India. A flexible approach to assessment, which takes success and failure in terms of the interplay of key parameters, can help to recognize specific areas of improvement and build upon them, to provide a greater sense of accomplishment and motivation over time.

References

Alley, Kelly D. 2002. *On the Banks of the Ganga: When Wastewater Meets a Sacred River*. Ann Arbor: University of Michigan Press.

Alley, K. D. 2014. "Ganga and Varanasi's Waste-water Management: Why Has It Remained Such an Intractable Problem?" *SANDRP South Asia Network* on *Dams, Rivers and People* (blog). Accessed July 14, 2018. https://sandrp. wordpress.com/2014/09/25/varanasis-ganga-wastewater-management-why-has-it-remained-such-an-intractable-problem/.

Alley, Kelly. 2015. "Rejuvenating the Ganga." *Global Water Forum,* July 13. Accessed July 14, 2018. http://www. globalwaterforum.org/2015/08/13/rejuvenating-the-ganga/.

Alley, Kelly D. 2016. Rejuvenating Ganga: Challenges and Opportunities in Institutions, Technologies and Governance. *Tekton: A Journal of Architecture, Urban Design and Planning* 3(1) March

Alley, Kelly D. , Jennifer Barr and Tarini Mehta. 2018. Infrastructure Disarray in the Clean Indian/Clean Ganga Campaigns." *Wiley Interdisciplinary Reviews: Water*. doi:10.1002/wat2.1310.

Amerasinghe, P., R. M. Bhardwaj, C. Scott, K. Jella, and F. Marshall. 2013. "Urban Wastewater and Agricultural Reuse Challenges in India." *IWMI Research Report* 147: 1–28.

Anand, Nikhil. 2017. *Hydraulic City: Water and the Infrastructures of Citizenship in Mumbai*. Durham: Duke University Press.

Arora, M., H. Malano, B. Davidson, R. Nelson, and B. George. 2015. "Interactions Between Centralized and Decentralized Water Systems in Urban Context: A Review." *Wiley Interdisciplinary*

Reviews: Water 2 (6): 623–634.

Bahinipati, Chandra Sekhar. 2017. "Coping Costs of Urban Water in Smart Cities in India: Status, Issues and Policy Lessons." Asian Cities Climate Change Resilience Network (ACCRN). The Rockefeller Foundation.

Barnes, J. 2014. "Mixing Waters: The Reuse of Agricultural Drainage Water in Egypt." *Geoforum* 57: 181–191.

Bear, Laura. 2015. *Navigating Austerity: Currents of Debt along a South Asian River.* Stanford: Stanford University press

Bjorkman, Lisa. 2015. *Pipe Politics. Contested Water: Embedded Infrastructures of Millenial Mumbai.* Durham: Duke University Press.

Budds, Jessica. 2008. "Whose Scarcity? The Hydrosocial Cycle and the Changing Waterscape of La Ligua River Basin, Chile." In *Contentious Geographies: Environment, Meaning, Scale*, edited by M. Goodman, M. Boykoff, and K. Evered, 59–68. Hampshire: Ashgate.

Cross, J. 2016. "Off the Grid: Infrastructure and Energy Beyond the Mains." In *Infrastructures and Social Complexity: A Companion,* edited by P. Harvey, C. Bruun Jensen, and A. Morita. New York: Routledge.198-209

Cullet, Philippe. 2017. "A Gathering Crisis: The Need for Groundwater Regulation." *The Hindu,* August 8, 2017, accessed July 14, 2018. http://

www.thehindu.com/opinion/op-ed/a-gathering-crisis-the-need-for-groundwater-regulation/article1944 6507.ece.

Dasgupta, Simanti. 2015. *Bits of Belonging: Information Technology, Water, and Neoliberal Governances in India*. Philadelphia: Temple University Press.

Fielding, Kelly D., Sara Dolnicar, and Tracy Schultz. 2018. "Public Acceptance of Recycled Water." *International Journal of Water Resources Development*. 34 (4) doi:10.1080/07900627.201 7.1419125.

Follmann (2014)

Forest, Ecology and Environment Secretariat. Government of Karnataka? Bengaluru Notification January 19, 2016.

Frijns, Jos, Heather M. Smith, Stijn Brouwer, Kenisha Garnett, Richard Elelman, and Paul Jeffrey. 2016. "How Governance Regimes Shape the Implementation of Water Reuse Schemes." *Water* 8: 605.

Gupta, Akhil. 2015. "An Anthropology of Electricity from the Global South." *Cultural Anthropology* 30 (4): 555–568.

Hurlimann, A., and J. McKay. 2007. "Urban Australians Using Recycled Water for Domestic Non-Potable Use—An Evaluation of the Attributes Price, Saltiness, Colour and Odour Using Conjoint Analysis." *Journal of Environ-* *mental Management* 83 (1): 93–104.

Jamwal, Priyanka, Bejoy K. Thomas, Sharachchandra Lele, and Veena Srinivasan. 2014. "Addressing Water Stress Through Wastewater Reuse: Complexities and Challenges in Bangalore, India." Proceedings of the Resilient Cities 2014 Congress.

Kontogianni, Areti, Ian H. Langford, Andreas Papandreou, and Mihalis S. Skourtos. 2003. "Social Preferences for Improving Water Quality: An Economic Analysis of Benefits from Wastewater Treatment." *Water Resources Management* 17 (5): 317–336.

Krishna Chaitanya, S. V., and S. V. Krishna. 2017. "What Drought? Check out IIT Madras, It's an Oasis." *Indian Express* May 11, 2017, accessed July 14, 2018. http://www.newindianexpress. com/cities/chennai/2017/may/11/ what-drought-check-out-iit-madras-its-an-oasis-1603523--1.html.

Kuttuva, P., S. Lele, and G. V. Mendez. 2018. "Decentralized Wastewater Systems in Bengaluru, India: Success or Failure?" *Water Economics and Policy* 4 (2): 1650043.Lienhoop Nele, Emad K. Al-Karablieh, Amer Z. Salman, Jaime A. Cardona. 2014. Environmental cost–benefit analysis of decentralised wastewater treatment and re-use: a case study of rural Jordan. *Water Policy* (16): 323–339

Linton, Jamie, and Jessica Budds. 2013. "The Hydrosocial Cycle: Defining and Mobilizing a Relational-Dialectical Approach to Water." *Geoforum.* (57): 170-180

Maurya, Nutan, Karthick Radhakrishnan, K. Alley, S. Das, and J. Barr. 2017. "A Review Report of the Decentralized Wastewater Treatment System (DEWATS) of Kachhpura Agra." Unpublished report. doi: 10.13140/RG.2.2.22748.28805.

Molinos-Senante, M., F. Hernández-Sancho, and R. Sala-Garrido. 2011. "Cost–Benefit Analysis of Water-Reuse Projects for Environmental Purposes: A Case Study for Spanish Wastewater Treatment Plants." *Journal of Environmental Management* 92 (12): 3091–3097.

Narain, Sunita. 2018. "Every Drop Matters. Opinion." *Down to Earth,* June 27.

Niti Aayog. *Composite Water Management Index: A Tool for Water Management.* June, 2018.

Pandey, Kundan. 2015. "AAP Government Announces Free Water, Cheap Electricity for Delhi Residents." *Down to Earth,* February 25, 2015.

Raghavendra, S. 2006. "Re-Examining the 'Low Water Tariff' Hypothesis: Lessons from Hyderabad, India." *Urban Water Journal* 3 (4): 235–247.

Ranganathan, M. 2014. "'Mafias' in the Waterscape: Urban Informality and Everyday Public Authority in Bangalore." *Water Alternatives* 7 (1): 89–105.

Ranganathan M. 2016. Rethinking Urban Water (In)formality. *Oxford Handbooks Online.* 2016-08-03. Oxford: Oxford University Press

Ravishankar, Chaya, Sunil Nautiyal, and Manasi Seshaiah. 2018. "Social Acceptance for Reclaimed Water Use: A Case Study in Bengaluru." *Recycling* 3: 4. doi:10.3390/recycling3010004.

Rohilla, Suresh Kumar, and Deblina Dwivedi. 2013. *Re-Invent, Recycle and Reuse-Toolkit on Decentralized Wastewater Management.* Delhi: Center for Science and Environment.

Roomratanapun, W. 2001. "Introducing Centralised Wastewater Treatment in Bangkok: A Study of Factors Determining Its Acceptability." *Habitat International* 25 (3): 359–371.

Roy, A., 2009. Why India Cannot Plan Its Cities: Informality, Insurgence and the Idiom of Urbanization. *Planning Theory* 8 (1), 76–87

Roy A. and A. Ong, eds. 2012. *Worlding Cities: Asian Experiments and the Art of Being Global.* Wiley-Blackwell

Sandrp. 2017. "DRP News Bulletin 16 October 2017: New Groundwater Guidelines threat to India's Water Lifeline." *SANDRP, South Asia Network on Dams, Rivers and People Blog.*

Sanghi, Rashmi, ed. 2014. *Our National River Ganga: Lifeline of Millions.* Switzerland: Springer.

Schwartz K, Luque MT, Rusca M, Ahlers R. 2015. (In)formality: the meshwork of water service provisioning. *Wiley Interdisciplinary Reviews: Water* (2): 31–36.

Sengupta, Sushmita. 2018. "At Least 200 Cities Are Fast Running out of Water." *Down to Earth*, March 31, 2018. http://www.downtoearth.org.in/news/bengaluru-beijing-mexico-city-and-istanbul-are-some-of-the-cities-that-are-headed-towards-day-zero-59984#.WrRr_-fLJAE.facebook.

Shah, Mihir. *A 21st Century Institutional Architecture for India's Water Reforms. Report Submitted by the Committee on Restructuring the CWC and CGWB.* July 2016.

Sovacooll, Benjamin K., and M. V. Ramana. 2015. "Back to the Future: Small Modular Reactors, Nuclear Fantasies, and Symbolic Convergence." *Science, Technology, & Human Values* 40 (1): 96–125.

Starkl, Marcus, Norbert Brunner, and Thor-Axel Stenström. 2017. Why Do Water and Sanitation Systems for the Poor Still Fail? Policy Analysis in Economically Advanced Developing Countries. *Environmental Science and Technology* 47, 6102–6110 Starkl, Markus, Josephine Anthony, Enrique Aymerich, Norbert Brunner, Caroline Chubilleau, Sukanya Das, Makarand M. Ghangrekar, Absar Ahmad Kazmi, Ligy Philip, and Anju Singh. 2018. "Interpreting Best Available Technologies More Flexibly: A Policy Perspective for Municipal Wastewater Management in India and Other Developing Countries." *Environmental Impact Assessment Review* 71: 132–141.

Suneethi, S., G. Keerthiga, R. Soundhar, M. Kanmani, T. Boobalan, D. Krithika, and L. Philip. 2015. "Qualitative Evaluation of Small Scale Municipal Wastewater Treatment Plants (WWTPs) in South India." *Water Practice and Technology* 10 (4): 711–719.

Swyngedouw, E. 2009. "The Political Economy and Political Ecology of the Hydrosocial Cycle." *Journal of Contemporary Water Research and Education* 142: 56–60.

Tare, V., and G. Roy. 2015. "The Ganga: A Trickle of Hope." In *Living Rivers, Dying Rivers: A Quest through India*, edited by R. Iyer. New Delhi, India: Oxford University Press.

Ulsrude, K., T. Winther, D. Palit, H. Rohracher, and J. Sandgren. 2011. "The Solar Transitions Research on Solar Mini-Grids in India: Learning from Local Cases of Innovative Socio-Technical Systems." *Energy for Sustainable Development* 15, no. 3 293-303 (September).

Vandewalle, Emily, and Wendy Jepson. 2015. "Mediating Water Governance: Point-of-Use Water Filtration Devices for Low-Income Communities along the US–Mexico Border." *GEO: Geography and Environment* 2(9): 107-121

Notes

1   The research for this paper was supported by the National Science Foundation, Cultural Anthropology program.

2   Additionally, this study finds that control of water begins to devolve toward the level of consumer control and these shifts can mean eventual changes in governance and in technological solutions (see Vandewalle and Jepson 2015).

3   In a study of Bangkok residents, Roomratanapun (2001) found that the level of acceptability for reuse projects declined when direct costs and changes in life style were involved. The study found that complex stimuli, such as cost-effectiveness and the convenience of the technology, tend to influence the degree of acceptability. Kontogianni et al. (2003) observed that those who were willing to pay for treated water believed in state investment for better water quality. They were also motivated by moral concerns linked to health and cultural issues, concern for future generations, and interest in environmental and educational issues.

4   There are many government reports and news items putting the estimate of untreated wastewater at around 70% of all wastewater generated in India. The most authoritative reports have been created by (1) the Centre for Science and Environment ("78% of sewage generated in India remains untreated" Down to Earth. DTE Staff, April 5, 2016); (2) the Central Pollution Control Board. Inventorization of Sewage Treatment Plants. March 2015; and (3) research reports such as Amerasinghe et al. (2013).

5   In Bangalore, Ravishankar, Nautiyal, and Seshaiah (2018) found that 67% of residents who were household owners were willing to buy reclaimed water, 20% were concerned about hygiene, and 33% of respondents lacked trust in the public agency with respect to water quality standards.

6   The potential for reuse also depends on the hydraulic and biochemical characteristics of the particular wastewater in question, making choice of technology an important determinant (Rohilla and Dwivedi 2013).

7   Directions of NGT order dated June 11, 2015, in the matter of OA No. 6/2012 & 300/2013, accessed July 14, 2018, http://delhi.gov.in/wps/wcm/connect/07be330048dbd704b6f9ff7a2b587979/ Directions_Clarifications_NGT_11.6.2015.pdf?MOD=AJPERES&lmod=-287594179.

8   According to the Ministry of Water resource's Ganga basin report "the mean annual replenishable groundwater in India as a whole has been assessed at 433 BCM per annum, of which about 202.5 billion cumec per annum (46.8%) lies in the states of the Ganga basin" (Groundwater Observation wells, accessed July 14, 2018, http://nihroorkee.gov.in/Gangakosh/ Water%20Resources/gwwells.htm).

9   Jamwal et al. (2014, 12) write, "Complexes of more than 50 apartments are required to install STPs and recycle and reuse all their effluents under a zero-liquid-discharge order by the KSPCB (CII 2014). Forest, Ecology and Environment Secretariat, Notification No FEE 316, EPC 2015, Bengaluru January 19, 2016"; in Delhi, the requirement is more provisional, with the Delhi Development Authority encouraging rather than requiring housing complexes to install recycling units (see Master Plan for Delhi—2021, Delhi Development Authority, draft compilation). In addition, Delhi Government offices, institutions, schools, and aided schools under the broad classification of Commercial/Industrial Category are eligible for 15% rebate on their total monthly bills, provided they adopt water harvesting and waste water recycling, http://www.delhi.gov.in/wps/wcm/connect/bef8998040c5c372b4b6be9bd169ec4a/ New+Water+Tariff.pdf?MOD=AJPERES&lmod=-312894429&CACHEID=bef8998040c5c37

2b4b6be9bd169ec4a; see also para 7 of No. 19 of 2003, [17/3/2003]—The Water (Prevention and Control of Pollution) Cess (Amendment) Act, 2003, http://www.moef.nic.in/sites/default/files/No%2036%201977_0.pdf.

10   Hurlimann and McKay (2007) have argued that policies for wastewater reuse depend on the acceptance by the community on the basis of the price, color, odor, and salt content of the recycled water.

11   Conversation on September 27, 2017.

12   After surveying studies that addressed the acceptability of water recycling schemes and the use of recycled water around the world, Fielding, Dolnicar, and Schultz (2018) found that: "(1) public outreach is critically important to the success of a project; (2) public outreach must be targeted to specific stakeholder groups and include both proactive marketing and general education of the public in water-related matters, emphasizing the benefits of recycled water specifically; (3) planners need to earn the public's trust by being transparent and involving experts; and (4) the timing of proposing a recycling project plays a role, with times of more obvious lack of water being optimal" (2018, 24). They could not assert any cross-cultural patterns showing the dominance of one variable or another playing a significant role in promoting acceptability.

13   The Delhi Jal Board is the primary government entity selling water in the National Capital Region. It sells the same water to householders, charging Rs. 5.27 per kiloliter for a supply up to 20 kiloliter per month. After this, the charge jumps to Rs. 26.36 per kiloliter for 20–30 kiloliter of usage per month and they add a sewage maintenance charge of 60% of that water volumetric charge. A large hotel company would pay up to Rs. 175 per kiloliter for the same kind of fresh or "pure" water from the Delhi Jal Board. A sliding scale on pricing surface water favors conservation and makes buyers more motivated to find cheaper water sources including recycled or reclaimed wastewater. Groundwater is generally cheaper, as it is priced by the energy required to extract it. Water tanker prices for water supply in unpiped or "unauthorized" zones are much higher than the greatest consumer use category and can go to Rs. 100–120 per kiloliter in crisis periods.

14   STPs are mandatory for industries in Tamil Nadu and Chennai under enforcement by the State Pollution Control Board. There is also a zero liquid discharge rule in Tamil Nadu and a prohibition against groundwater use, both applying to industries. There are CETPs for small industries that operate as a cluster.

15   There are also abruptly administered national policies that create effects on approaches to sanitation. These include the policies imposed over night by the central administration that cause long-term ripples in society and economy, such as demonetization and the GST.

16   Draft guidelines for issuance of No Objection Certificate (NOC) for ground water withdrawal. Central Ground Water Authority, Ministry of Water Resources, RD & GR, Government of India. http://mowr.gov.in/draft-guidelines-issuance-no-objection-certificate-noc-ground-water-withdrawal. October 2017.

17   Cullet (2017) notes, "It [the new bill] is based on the recognition of the unitary nature of water, the need for decentralised control over groundwater and the necessity to protect it at the aquifer level. The Bill is also based on legal developments that have taken place in the past few decades. ... The Bill also builds on the decentralisation mandate that is already enshrined in general legislation but has not been implemented effectively as far as groundwater is concerned and seeks to give regulatory control over groundwater to local user."

18 Delhi Jal Board Water Tariff revised February 1, 2018.

19 Report of Effluent Usage at STPs, Delhi Jal Board, unpublished document. September 2017 (provided upon our request).

20 Forest, Ecology and Environment Secretariat Notification No. FEE 316 EPC 2015, Bengaluru, January 19, 2016; Tamil Nadu??

21 Interview with Dr. Ligy Philip, IIT-M, October 5, 2017.

22 Interview with Manager of Engineering Department, Marriott Renaissance Hotel and Conference Center, October 14, 2017.

23 Private water tankers hike prices by nearly 40pc as Bengaluru's water crisis deepens *Think Change India*, April 3, 2017, accessed July 14, 2018, https://yourstory.com/2017/04/water-crisis-hike-price/.

India's Search for Economic Prosperity and Global Power

Kanta Murali[1]

Assistant Professor, Department of Political Science, University of Toronto
kanta.murali@utoronto.ca

Ayres, Alyssa. 2018. *Our Time Has Come: How India Is Making Its Place in the World*. New York: Oxford University Press.

Joshi, Vijay. 2017. *India's Long Road: The Search for Prosperity*. New York: Oxford University Press.

Sinha, Aseema. 2016. *Globalizing India: How Global Rules and Markets Are Shaping India's Rise to Power*. Cambridge: Cambridge University Press.

Twenty-seven years after the extensive economic reforms of 1991, India stands at an inflexion point. On the one hand, more than two-and-a-half decades of rapid economic growth has firmly placed it in the ranks of the world's emerging powers. On the other, India remains plagued by a variety of domestic problems and challenges—a quarter of its population remains mired in extreme poverty, public services remain woeful, economic inequality and exclusion along a variety of dimensions continues to rise, crony capitalism and corruption abound, the decay of numerous public institutions is all too evident, and the country has some of the highest rates of environmental pollution in the world.

Over the last four years, India has also, arguably, been witnessing one of the lowest points in its democratic history with the sharp rise of majoritarian and illiberal politics. How should we reconcile these apparently contradictory trends, between India's growth and its persistent problems? What do these trends mean for India's economic and geopolitical future? What factors are likely to affect the pace, scale, and nature of India's ongoing global integration? How is the interaction between the domestic and international realms likely to play out in this process of transformation?

Three recent accounts—Vijay Joshi's *India's Long Road*, Alyssa Ayres' *Our Time Has Come*, and Aseema

---

1   I would like to thank IPP's book review editor, Arzan Tarapore, for his useful suggestions on an earlier draft.

Sinha's *Globalizing India*—offer varying insights into those questions. India's economic liberalization forms the central backdrop of all three books but each of the accounts emphasizes different aspects of the country's transformation—Joshi offers a comprehensive evaluation of India's economic performance since independence, Ayres traces the evolution of India's geopolitical role in this period, and Sinha meticulously explores the interplay between international and domestic factors in India's marked global economic integration after the late 1990s. Despite the distinct analytical focus of each author—economic performance broadly for Joshi, foreign policy for Ayres, and global economic integration for Sinha—there is common ground in their discussions and bringing the three books in conversation with each other offers useful insights. All three books view economic liberalization as fundamental to India's global rise; all three recognize, though to varying degrees, the interaction (indeed, tension at certain points) between the international and domestic realms in the process of transformation; and all three offer carefully considered analyses that have implications for India's future prospects.

Such broad overlap in their discussions aside, the books differ in important ways. Ayres is the most optimistic about India's prospects, suggesting that economic growth is likely to continue and underpin the country's rise as a global power. Joshi is far more skeptical of India's economic prospects, suggesting that "high-quality" growth, which has eluded India to date, would demand an unprecedented raft of policy reforms. In contrast to those accounts, Sinha places greater priority on international economic institutions and trade rules as the primary catalysts for changes within the Indian state, the domestic private sector, and in state–business relations after the late 1990s. In the remainder of this essay, I outline the key arguments of each book, and offer critical analyses of how each adds to our understanding of India's economic and foreign policy prospects.

Charting India's Geopolitical Rise

In *Our Time Has Come*, Alyssa Ayres argues that India is unmistakably on the path to becoming a global power—but, for a variety of reasons including India's own foreign policy history and numerous domestic challenges, she expects this rise to occur in a "cautious" fashion. Ayres views India's economic liberalization in 1991 and the impressive economic growth that followed over the next two-and-a-half decades as the primary basis for India's rise on the global stage. Alongside economic growth, she points out that India has been steadily building its strategic capacity, adding to its leverage. In many ways, the book unambiguously celebrates India's growing geopolitical ambitions; a clear point of contrast with Joshi's book discussed later in the article.

The book is divided into three sections; the first part examines India's foreign policy history until economic liberalization, the second part focuses on the transition on India's global role since the 1990s, and the third part evaluates India's future prospects. As India grows in economic stature on the world stage, she suggests that India simultaneously, and paradoxically, sees itself as a "great civilization with much to offer the world" while often seeking to "remain aloof of world entanglements" (65). This remains the basis of India's foreign policy thinking as it attempts to transition from a "balancing" to a "leading" power under the Modi government; a process she suggests that is a work in progress and will take time.

While the rise of India's global power can be seen in various domains, Ayres points out that India has traditionally been a cautious actor on the world stage, though the preference for caution has begun to weaken in recent times. Ayres expects India to retain some of its habitual caution even as it attempts to become a leading power, due to constraints imposed by geopolitics—particularly China's and Pakistan's strategies, India's own inheritance of nonalignment and nonintervention, and the contentious nature of its domestic politics, which she suggests constraints the country's international diplomacy. An element of suspicion of foreign involvement in India's affairs, which was at its height during Indira Gandhi's time in office in the 1970s, continues to be evident, and she cites examples such as the Foreign Contribution Regulatory Act in this regard.

The final section focuses on India's future trajectory along two lines—India's attempts to build alternative institutions at the international level

that give it greater voice and changes in the Indian economy aimed at higher growth. Given the constraints that it has faced in gaining a greater role in established multilateral institutions, Ayres suggests that India has actively been working to develop alternative institutions with other BRICS countries, Indian Ocean countries, as well as in Asia as part of its "Look East" policy. Interestingly, and perhaps unconventionally, Ayres discusses India's dominance in the International Cricket Council as an example of how a powerful India might act in the future.

Ayres recognizes that India's future prospects are predicated on continued economic growth. While identifying several current constraints to continued economic progress, she seems to be optimistic regarding India's efforts to remove some of these constraints, such as initiatives to make the manufacturing sector more competitive. The book concludes with a variety of specific recommendations for how the United States should work with a rising India such as "approach India as a joint venture partner, not an ally in waiting" (216), "bring India into economic organizations" (220), and "develop stronger bilateral trade ties" (221). In the final analysis, "India, as a major rising power of Asia, should be better understood and better appreciated on its own terms—as a competitiveness issue for U.S. economic and business interests, and as a matter of the demands of the new global diplomacy in which all of Asia plays a much more pivotal role" (242).

Domestic Factors and India's Global Ambitions: Case for Greater Pessimism

The change in India's geopolitical ambitions and the country's own understanding of its place in the world after the 1990s is effectively documented in Ayres' book. Her book is a cogent, accessible, and thorough account of India's geopolitical ascendancy since the 1990s. While the book convincingly highlights the various mechanisms through which India's attempted transformation to a leading power is occurring, the optimistic and celebratory tone with which it views these changes can be called into question for several reasons. For a start, Ayres automatically seems to assume that India's goal of becoming a leading power is a worthy one, and she neglects normative discussion of any potential costs of such ambition. As Joshi points out in his book, India's deliberate pursuit of global power comes with clear trade-offs in that it shifts the efforts of the state away from numerous domestic development challenges. Indeed, as seen elsewhere through history, foreign policy expansionism and great power ambitions can potentially be used to divert attention from major domestic failings. The potential for such diversionary tactics certainly exists, given the immense scope of India's domestic social, political, and economic challenges.

Second, Ayres underestimates the nature and significance of the links between domestic politics and India's foreign policy, especially under the current BJP government. Ayres clearly identifies domestic politics as one of the constraints that leads to India's cautious approach on the world stage but she seems to view domestic politics primarily as a check on the speed of India's global ascendance. Rather, the case can be made that the links between foreign policy and domestic politics may be more complex. Under the current BJP government, whose activities and pronouncements related to the international arena are frequently used as examples through the book, foreign policy appears to be a key part of a broader political model that combines, among other aspects, muscular nationalism, majoritarianism, and illiberal politics. From the point of view of the quality, inclusiveness, and openness of Indian democracy, there is little to celebrate in that political model. In that sense, India's current global power ambitions are hardly benign and may have negative implications for democracy in India.

Third, and related to the point above, there appears to be a tension between notions of continuity and change in Ayres' treatment of foreign policy under the current government. She makes the case that an element of continuity in Indian foreign policy can be seen across successive Indian governments and this is demonstrated by the fact that ideas such as sovereignty and nonintervention continue to play a guiding role. But the book also draws on several examples under the Modi government, which seem to imply that the BJP's approach to foreign policy under Modi is different than those of previous governments. It is unclear whether these examples merely reflect stylistic differences with previous governments or whether there is a qualitative shift in India's foreign policy doctrine under Modi.

Fourth, Ayres' optimism of India's future economic prospects seems to downplay some of the weaknesses in India's current growth model—particularly the lack of domestic inclusiveness—and it underestimates the scale of the challenges that India needs to tackle to maintain rapid growth. She offers evidence from efforts to improve manufacturing and the case of the auto industry as one that now thrives despite various weaknesses in the past. To a certain extent, her analysis of the improved fortunes of the auto sector finds resonance with Sinha's analysis of the textile sector outlined later in this article. However, as other studies of political economy of India (e.g., Drèze and Sen 2013; Kohli 2012) point out, India's growth has not been inclusive enough; a point also emphasized strongly by Joshi. Joshi argues that changes since 1991 can be characterized as a "partial reform model" and continued adherence to this model is unlikely to achieve what he considers sustained "high-quality" growth. Given that Ayres' expectations about India's future foreign policy prospects are predicated on the country's continued economic success, these weaknesses inherent in the current growth model could potentially act as a more significant constraint on India's global ambitions than the book accounts for.

India's Economic Performance: The Past, the Present, and the Future

In several ways, Vijay Joshi's comprehensive and meticulously detailed account of India's economic performance acts as a sobering and refreshing corrective to the hype that has frequently surrounded the country's economic prospects over the last decade. Joshi's central argument is that "with 'business-as-usual' policies India will be hard put to achieve high-quality and enduring per-capita growth of even 6 per cent a year, let alone 8 per cent a year, which would be necessary for it to become a prosperous nation in the next quarter century" (5). To become a prosperous nation, India requires radical reforms along various lines.

In spelling out this argument, Joshi begins by emphasizing the enormity of the task that lies in front of India in order to achieve 'high-quality' growth, which refers to inclusive and environmentally friendly growth, and why he believes that India is likely to face an uphill task without radical changes. The reforms that began in the 1990s were effective but are now running out of steam and could only be considered partial and incomplete in the first place. The mode of policy change—"reforms by stealth"—is also unlikely to bring about the deep changes necessary to ensure high-quality growth. Further, India's rapid growth in the first decade of the 2000s was propelled by a highly liquid and expanding world economy and that such a "benign global environment looks very unlikely to return any time soon" (7). A weak government sector and crony capitalism additionally compound existing challenges.

Interestingly, Joshi departs from standard neoliberal analyses of India's economic performance and prospects by arguing that more liberalization is necessary but will not be sufficient to ensure and sustain "high-quality" growth. This is because the Indian state "no longer performs its core functions effectively" (7). A central weakness of the current growth model for Joshi, thus, lies in the nature of India's state–market relationship. According to him, India has not found the correct balance between state and market to achieve "high-quality" growth. This, in turn, necessitates the need for radical reform of the state and the state–market relationship. As an interesting aside, and a clear contrast with Ayres in this regard, Joshi argues that deliberate pursuit of great power status by India would be "unwise, if not foolish," given the scale of the domestic challenges that remain.

After offering a preview of the main argument, the book is divided into five parts. Part 1 offers an evaluation of India's economic performance since independence, Part 2 focuses on the challenge of growth, Part 3 examines stability and inclusion, Part 4 focuses on India's political economy, and Part 5 discusses future prospects and evaluates the performance of the Modi government on various measures required to ensure rapid and inclusive growth.

In examining the history of India's economic performance, Joshi suggests that India's disappointing growth performance between 1950 and 1980 was primarily due to the fact that "Indian policymakers acted with a mistaken conception of the role of the state" (19). Joshi confirms that growth acceleration after 1980 has been most pronounced in the service sector, which also saw total factor productivity grow much faster than agriculture or industry. Unlike cases in East Asia, India has not exploited the gains associated with shifting labor out of low productivity farming. For Joshi, the marked weakness in terms of employment generation lies firmly with the nature of labor laws in India and he suggests that radical reforms in terms of flexibility, severance, and unemployment benefits and job-search training are required.

In terms of inclusion, Joshi highlights India's gross underperformance in health and education. The problem in his view is that it has historically been taken for granted in India that the state should deliver education and healthcare. Solving this problem involves a much more extensive role for the private sector; while the state should ensure access to health and education for the poorest, the delivery of services needs to be shifted more significantly to the private sector. Two major trends—"social and political awakening" and "institutional decay"—have characterized Indian democracy for Joshi in recent years and have had effects on the state's performance. Joshi also highlights the weakness in state capacity through a lengthy discussion on petty and grand corruption as well as crony capitalism in India. The glaring lack of state capacity and accountability, thus, highlights the need for a radical reorientation of the involvement of the state in the economy.

In the final part of the book, Joshi reiterates the inadequacy of India's current "partial reforms model" and the need for sweeping reforms to achieve higher prosperity. He also includes an interesting evaluation of first two years of the performance of the Modi government. How has the Modi government performed? Joshi suggests the answer is "mixed at best" (309).

Politics and the Radical Reform Agenda

*I*ndia's *Long Road* is a comprehensive, accessible, balanced, and nuanced account that is an important reading for anyone interested in India's political economy. The central argument of the book is persuasive and Joshi marshals strong evidence in support of his call for a radical reform agenda. Joshi's emphasis on the state and its role in India's future prospects is also a refreshing departure from typical analyses on the Indian economy written by economists. Despite these strengths, there are a few aspects, mainly related to the political arena, that the book downplays and could consider more substantially.

The book views the relationship between state and private business in India in a relatively simplistic fashion. In particular, the tone of the book often juxtaposes a weak and inefficient state with a dynamic private sector, and the private sector seems to be treated

as a passive recipient of economic policy decisions. There is little doubt that private sector dynamism has been a central theme of India's economic acceleration after 1991 and the state in India has exhibited growing weakness in several areas in this period. However, at least three aspects point to the need for greater complexity in the treatment of state–business relations in India, and suggest that it is important to go beyond the venal state versus passive private sector narrative.

For a start, private capital's role in broader trends of cronyism and corruption that have characterized the post-liberalization environment in India cannot be downplayed. Second, the period since the 1980s has generally been marked by a closer relationship between state and business. Arguably, the connections between the political and economic elite in India are closer now than at any other point in Indian history. Importantly, both the structural and instrumental leverage of business have grown in the post-liberalization period. This growth in leverage is evident in several arenas—for example, the growing presence of businesspersons in parliament and state legislatures, and the increased scope of activities and influence of business associations in policy arenas. As such, Indian business is not a passive recipient of policies currently and it also bears some responsibility for trends of cronyism and corruption, which Joshi identifies as a central weakness of the state.

Third, the book tends to treat the state and the private sector as somewhat monolithic and uniform in their capacities. In this regard, Sinha's analysis, which is discussed in the next section, offers a contrasting viewpoint. Importantly, her analysis, backed by in-depth case studies of the textile and pharmaceutical sectors, suggests a significant reconfiguration of the business–state relationship in the realm of trade policy after the late 1990s. Her account, albeit one that is narrower in scope than Joshi's book, shows that in response to certain imperatives of globalization, the Indian state and private business came much closer together after the late 1990s and actively collaborated and consulted with each other in formulating a coherent response that resulted in greater global integration. Importantly, for Sinha, the Indian state "facilitated deeper integration than expected and has been at the forefront of change in trade policy and economic institutions as well as markets" (Sinha, 274). According to her, we are witnessing a "new developmental state" in India, "one that combines statism with multiple plural interests" (Sinha, 281). What her book implies for Joshi's analysis is that state capacity in India is very uneven and the state's willingness to collaborate with the private sector may differ along different policy dimensions. Moreover, both the state and the private sector in India may be more fragmented and diverse than Joshi's analysis assumes.

In terms of the links between Indian democracy and its economic model, Joshi's book primarily treats the former as affecting the latter. However, not surprisingly, economic liberaliza-tion has also had effects on Indian democracy. In particular, the lack of economic inclusiveness has contributed to the development of what Kohli refers to as a "two-track democracy" where the poor are primarily consigned to the electoral sphere while the elite dominate policymaking. Exclusionary economic trends have also meant that electoral mobilization continues to occur primarily along lines of identity and other symbolic aspects. As such, there may be a more complex two-way link between democracy and economic performance than the book accounts for.

The book tends to focus mainly on technocratic solutions such as cash transfers or basic income in the context of inclusion and social protection. However, welfare measures in many parts of the world have come about as the result of contentious, bottom-up politics placing pressure on states. As such, an active civil society and social movements that place pressure on the state to deliver may be central to trends of inclusion, not simply a restriction of the scope of the state's activities and transfer of delivery to the private sector that Joshi focuses on. Finally, while the case for a radical reform agenda is compelling, the book is largely silent about what the catalysts for such change might be. Joshi very briefly considers the role of the middle class as well as that of state governments at the end of the book, but a more substantial discussion on these potential catalysts would be useful.

The Interplay of International and Domestic Factors in India's Global Integration

Joshi's book follows a significant portion of the scholarship in Indian political economy that tends to view India's transformation as well as its economic future primarily through the lens of national or domestic variables. The scholarship has largely focused on the role of internal economic changes in driving India's global transformation. In contrast, Aseema Sinha in *Globalizing India* moves away from "methodological nationalism" and analyzes the joint interaction of global factors and domestic factors in a more complex manner. In doing so, she develops a "Global Design-in-Motion framework" and "starts with a 'second image reversed' argument" that focuses on how international variables affect domestic politics. She goes on to examine which specific aspects of globalization (rules or markets) shape and change Indian preferences and interests toward global integration.

The empirical puzzle that Sinha focuses on relates to India's rapid global economic integration after the late 1990s, specifically in the realms of trade and multilateral engagement. Sinha suggests that a paradigmatic shift began occurring in the late 1990s. Catalyzed primarily by a change in the global trade regime and the formation of the WTO in 1995 in particular, India witnessed substantial and rapid trade liberalization, and began to assertively participate in multilateral forums after the late 1990s. Focusing on this marked shift af-

ter the late 1990s, Sinha's book asks how India achieved rapid global integration, and analyzes the factors that propelled and facilitated this integration.

To address this central question, the book draws on in-depth empirical evidence from two sectors—pharmaceuticals and textiles. The book includes eight chapters. Chapter 1 sets the stage for the analysis and offers a brief preview of the argument, while Chapter 2 elaborates on the theoretical framework. Chapter 3 meticulously documents the changing nature of tradecraft and state capacity in India necessitated by changes in the global trade regime. Chapters 4–6 include empirical evidence from case studies of the pharmaceutical and textile sectors. After outlining the changes in these two sectors, Chapter 7 addresses the role of market and nonmarket mechanisms in driving these changes, and Chapter 8 concludes.

In answering what propelled India's substantial and deep global integration after the late 1990s, the book highlights the critical role played by international institutions and rules in transforming the Indian state, the private sector, and in affecting the nature of state–business relations. The catalyst for change in India's trade policies was external effects related to the WTO as well as global markets and geopolitics. These external levers, in turn, initiated "changes in state capacity and a new tradecraft" (15). After the loss of two major cases at the WTO in 1998, "India's trade policy regime changed radically in the late 1990s (after 1998)" (15). The nature of changes were extensive, and involved transformations in policies, the policymaking process, and state/institutional capacity. In addition, "reformist woodwork politicians" emerged with reformist bureaucrats disrupting vested interests, and new institutions, new collaborations, and new coalitions in support of trade reform were forged. Importantly, global changes resulted in the state collaborating more closely and actively with business.

Through what mechanisms did global factors transform India's domestic political economy? Sinha points to three global factors—geopolitics, global markets, and the WTO. Geopolitics, and the changing balance of power, created new sovereignty costs and changed the external environment for India. These changes resulted in a pro-U.S. shift and a wariness of China, and were the initial necessary conditions for domestic policy change. Such systemic factors combined with new opportunities and threats arising from global markets, which mobilized private sector actors as well as state actors to design new policies and institutions to deal with external changes. The third set of influences arose from global institutions, specifically the WTO, which generated nonmarket effects, pushed against policy autonomy, and resulted in onerous transaction and implementation costs that catalyzed new domestic responses and capacities.

In addition to driving domestic changes in policies, the policymaking process, and state capacity, the process of external integration also changed the nature of coalitions and interests domestically. Global changes disrupted vested interests and coalitions that favored protectionism and, importantly, "new winners and incipient reformers emerged from the woodwork within both within the state and the private sector" (19). In addition, new losers were unable to mobilize the state. For Sinha, "more coherent and strong actions by Indian policy and private actors at the global level ... are the consequence not the cause of global integration" (19).

Sinha marshals extensive empirical evidence from a variety of sources, including interviews, newspaper archives, and a variety of primary sources to support her argument. She offers a detailed analysis of how global integration played out in the pharmaceutical and textile sectors, which support her claim of the causal role of global factors in driving domestic changes.

State, Business, and Globalization

In many ways, Sinha's incisive and empirically meticulous analysis contributes significantly to the current political economy literature. For a start, as mentioned earlier, Sinha's book successfully accomplishes her aim of moving away from 'methodological nationalism' and she makes a convincing theoretical and empirical case for analyzing the joint effect of global and domestic factors in certain questions of Indian political economy.

A second contribution involves her treatment of the reforms process. A bulk of the political economy scholarship tends to view economic reforms process as one, continuous process that began in 1991 (or for some scholars, in the 1980s). The scholarship also often tends to conflate various policy dimensions involved in India's economic liberalization. Moreover, following Jenkins (1999), numerous studies characterize the process of reforms as incremental and carried out by "stealth." In contrast, Sinha highlights the distinct nature of "second generation reforms" in the area of trade policy, which in her view were extensive (not incremental) and rapid. This is a significant contrast to Joshi's general description of the reforms process. As such, her study implies that the Indian reforms process is potentially uneven in terms of speed and scope along different policy dimensions, and disaggregating reforms along different policy dimensions is likely to be a useful exercise.

A third contribution of her book is the nuanced treatment of the state and the state–business relationship. In contrast to accounts that discuss a secular decline in state capacity in India over the last few decades, the Indian state in Sinha's analysis played a major role in facilitating global integration. In that sense, her analysis, in contrast to Joshi's, suggests that the state might still be able to play a positive role in facilitating development in certain policy realms. Indeed, she suggests that there is evidence of a new developmental state in India, at least in the two sectors she analyzes, which has sufficient capacity to propel change and enjoys a close relationship with the private sector. Moreover, she suggests that this new developmental state is distinctive in combining "statism

with multiple plural interests" (281). While emphasizing close relations between state and business fostered by greater global integration, Sinha is also careful to recognize that both the state and the private sector in India are fragmented and diverse; interests within each are not monolithic.

Apart from these strengths, Sinha's analysis leads to certain questions that the book does not address squarely. Sinha's book is defined in scope—it examines the realm of trade policy and it draws significantly on empirical evidence from the textile and pharmaceutical sectors. In the realm of external economic integration and in these two sectors, the state comes across as relatively effective and as enjoying considerable capacity. Yet, as Sinha recognizes but does not elaborate, state capacity is very uneven and indeed weak in many other areas. What explains why the Indian state is more effective in some realms than others? As such, the unevenness of state capacity suggests that the Indian state is not so much a new developmental state as Sinha classifies it, but a state that exhibits pockets of developmental efficacy in certain realms in the midst of general weakness and inefficiency. Moreover, this raises the question of whether trade policy is relatively unique. In particular, did the technocratic nature of trade policy insulate the state to a certain extent from "mass politics"?

Finally, throughout the book, Sinha paints a positive picture of the state–business relationship and ability of a close relationship in particular to effect positive change. In contrast to accounts such as Joshi's, there is little discussion of the negative consequences of a close business–state relationship in terms of cronyism or corruption. This leads to broader questions on the state–business relationship in India. What factors determine whether a close relationship between state and business in India is likely to be developmental or descend into cronyism?

Conclusion: Internal and External Drivers of Reform

The three books reviewed offer different views on India's prospects for the future. They each also offer a different analysis of the drivers of India's geopolitical rise and economic growth, and the analyses complement each other. Thus, Ayres trumpets India's global rise and judges that its domestic economic foundations will keep reforming sufficiently to meet its growing needs. Joshi, meanwhile, argues that "high-quality"—more rapid and inclusive—economic growth will demand radical reforms, especially in the state–market relationship. And

Sinha adds that, in fact, international institutional changes have prompted the Indian state to lead extensive and rapid reforms, at least in some sectors. As these three volumes show, India's economic and geopolitical rise depend on a very complex interplay of domestic and international factors, and of the state and market—no single solution or pathway of reform will sustain India's burgeoning requirements.

References

Drèze, Jean, and Amartya Sen. 2013. *An Uncertain Glory: India and Its Contradictions.* Princeton, NJ: Princeton University Press.

Jenkins, Rob. 1999. *Democratic Politics and Economic Reform in India.* Cambridge: Cambridge University Press.

Kohli, Atul. 2012. *Poverty Amid Plenty in the New India.* Cambridge: Cambridge University Press.

www.ingramcontent.com/pod-product-compliance
Lightning Source LLC
Chambersburg PA
CBHW081647270326
41933CB00018B/3378